To Barbara, Jud, and Nancy

The Obvious Isn't™... in Baseball

Hidden Things You Never Knew About Baseball

Like Why Isn't it called Batball?
or
Why Did Many Historians
Get its Origins Wrong?

By
Winston J. Perez

© 2021 - 2023, Winston J. Perez

2nd Edition Release: August 8, 2023
Published by Shutter House Publishing

Inquiries:
149 S. Barrington Ave., #413
Los Angeles, CA 90049

Website: www.theobviousisnt.com or
www.conceptmodeling.com

Content is also derived from my book *Concerning the Nature and Structure of Concept* (Copyright 2017) Released: January, 2020. Content from this book is also taken from *The Obvious Isn't… in Baseball. Why Baseball Comes From the USA. Not Europe* (Copyright 2021) Content is also taken from *The Obvious Isn't…* podcast: Part I released October 30, 2020; Part II January 29, 2021.

All rights reserved, including the right of reproduction in whole or in part in any form. No part of this book may be reproduced in any form without the permission of the author. No claim is made for the text version of "Who is on First?" first performed by Abbott and Costello in 1938—only fair use and transformative use is claimed to make a point about our use of words.

No part of this publication may be reproduced, stored in a retrieval system, or transmitted in any form or by any means—electronic, mechanical, photocopying, recording, or otherwise—without the prior permission of the publisher or author in accordance with the provisions of the Copyright, Designs and Patents Act 1976 or under the terms of any license permitting limited copying issued by the Copyright Licensing Agency.

For information, special requests or orders, email here:
info@conceptmodeling.com

Library of Congress Control Number: 2022916983
Perez, Winston J.

Printed in The United States

The Obvious Isn't…in Baseball: Hidden Things You Never Knew About Baseball
ISBN: 979-8-9864236-0-9

Distributed by:
Shutter House Publishing
Attn: Winston Perez's *The Obvious Isn't…*
149 S. Barrington Ave. #413
Los Angeles, CA 90049

"Ideas and concepts are two separate things. In fact they are housed in two separate worlds."

—Winston Perez
Concerning the Nature and Structure of Concept

i. Acknowledgments

I want to acknowledge some people that rock: John Lundin, Hillary S. Zilz, and Greta Jernstedt. There is a smart man and huge baseball fan, Lance Bradford. The ever-cool Leo Nitzberg. Great Dodger fan Chris. Then there is the awesome Oscar winner, Nick Reed. There is also Joseph Scott, Thomas Locke, Tucker Tooley, and Jerry Bottomley. Also, I want to mention friends whose support was invaluable: Shirin Drost, Felipe Lulli, Ray DeCardenas, Ramon Tello, Kevin Stein, Richard Loria, Larry, Adele, Julia, Faribors Moravi, Fr. Paul Donlan, Jimmy Escobar, Phil Guye, Alise Guye, Efrem, Michael George, Michael Saltzman, Leland Phillips, Greg Horangic, and Alex Escobar. (As well as others I will have to thank personally.)

I also include people we miss: Bob Drabkin, Steven, Michael Stroot, Paul Simmons, Joe McPhearson, Paul Behrend, Jim Eastep, and of course, Donald, Merch and Pesky. Always.

Also, as I mention in the book, I could not have done some of this work without the work and research of David Block, John Thorn, and many other historians and writers listed throughout this book.

Table of Contents

i. Acknowledgements ... vi
ii. Game Day Introduction ... ix

Part I

1. The What, the How, and the Why ... 1
2. Simple Enough, a Baseball Versus a Softball ... 5
3. Baseball? What's Up with That? ... 9
4. Attributes. And Brady's Home Team Advantage ... 15
5. Relationships And Yes, Disruptive Tech in Baseball ... 25
6. The Once Hidden Concept at the Core of Baseball ... 33

Part II

Introduction to Part II ... 48

7. Why Concept Matters, and Why Baseball Origin Research Is At Risk ... 49

Seventh Inning Stretch

Who's On Third? No, He's on First? ... 61

Part II Continued

8. Base, As Not in "*Base*-Ball" but Baseball ... 65
9. Abbott and Costello Show Us a Bear of a Problem ... 83
10. The Description of Rounders in *The Boy's Own Book*, Second Edition, 1828, Is "False Advertising" ... 89
11. Tag this—The Origin of All of It ... 107

Part III

12. The Twist in Where American Baseball Really Comes From ... 115
13. Gloves: USA 1—Europe 0 ... 121
14. Bases: USA 2—Europe 0 ... 123
15. Baseballs: USA 3—Europe 0 ... 129

Part III Continued

16. Baseball Bats: USA 4—Europe 0	135
17. Strikes: USA 5—Europe 0	145
18. Pitching: USA 6—Europe 0	151
19. Stickball: USA 7—Europe 0	155
20. 1884: The Biggest Pitch of All	163
21. Four Foul Balls	167
22. Graphic Proof	173
23. Sound Proof	177
24. Batball? Oh Yeah! Proof!	181
25. One Number Above Baseball Analytics	189

Appendix

I. William Wheaton's Game-Changer Interview: "How Baseball Began—A Member of the Gotham Club of Fifty Years Ago Tells About It." *San Francisco Examiner*, Nov. 27, 1887	195
II. Tudor Fantasy Baseball	199
III. Illustrations	215
IV. References & Book Sources	216
V. End Notes	219
VI. Baseball Concept Model Can Be Found In Winston's Concept Modeling Master Course	221

ii. Game Day Introduction

Here is a look at our playing field, so to speak.

The discipline—what I call concept modeling—that I use in this book to deconstruct baseball is also used for movies in Hollywood, technology, science, and businesses. Anything and everything, actually. Most of you reading this probably have never heard of concept modeling, much less why or how it could apply to baseball. Let me briefly explain it and then get on with our deep dive into baseball—for fans and even for nonfans, who may not know how baseball is already a significant part of their lives.

Think of baseball in these terms: It is a competition that sports teams try to win. But as sports entertainment, it is about showcasing athletic skills within a live competition that can also extract the heart and fighting spirit of players and teams. It can showcase the nature of competition itself—the fight, the struggle to win, and the glory of victory.

Baseball also shines light and provides insights into a million other hidden things—personal things—for individuals fighting their own battles in daily life. Baseball players can show us an example of how to handle and perform at our best while under maximum pressure. We even see the lessons of baseball captured forever in sayings that translate perfectly into our life experience. You would be hard-pressed to find anyone who has not used baseball terms and analogies. Phrases such as the following: *Watch out for a curve ball. Aim for the fences.* Even nonfans can connect to the deeper side of baseball. Baseball offers us its own philosophy of sorts.

But stop and think. Did you notice anything? Nothing of what I wrote in the previous paragraph was actually about a physical thing like a ball or bat even though they represented the results of something physical. You cannot pick up a *curve ball* the way you could a bat, a glove, or even a baseball. Likewise, you cannot touch a *victory*; you can only experience it. But, amazingly, as fans we can share in that experience through the *victories* achieved by our favorite hometown team. There is a kind of emotional transference delivered instantly from a team to its fans that is not physical, and yet they truly feel it—a joy, a pride.

So what does all this mean? It means that baseball has both a physical nature and an abstract nature to it. My work in deconstructing the abstract nature of things involves a deep dive into essence—such as baseball's essence—to reveal the hidden secrets within, even in things we already know very well. Deconstruction in both the abstract and physical worlds can happen because it is the hidden abstract world that dictates how the physical world works.

It also means that we can use the abstract world to dive deeper into baseball than ever before. Amazingly, much of the nature of the abstract world actually lies within the obvious, so don't let that fool you. Hidden there are secrets that have always been there to discover; we just needed to know how and where to look. So expect some surprises that you can test on your baseball friends.

All of the above also proves that it is the abstract nature of the sport that connects it to things outside of baseball. One does not have to love baseball to love what it can teach about life and success itself. Cool!

Here's a twist: my work centers on how the abstract world works. Amazingly, a concept model I did on baseball back in 2006 was what led me to a far deeper understanding of how the abstract world actually works. It confirmed a discovery I made in 1989 and opened my eyes to how stuff in the abstract world can teach us more about how and why physical things—such as balls, bats, and bases—actually work. A baseball bat is a physical thing. But the essence of a *baseball bat* is something entirely different—it is not something we can physically touch. Amazingly, there is a way we can dig into that abstract nature and see new insights—fun stuff—and something that gives us deeper appreciation of this glorious sport. Oh yeah!

Let me also state this with emphasis: I could not have done this book, especially the rounders section, without the great work of baseball historian David Block and others. But I especially credit David and his seminal book, *Baseball Before We Knew It: A Search for the Roots of the Game*.[1]

Also, one proof is based on an important research finding by John Thorn, captured in *Baseball in the Garden of Eden*.[2] I did not find Thorn's evidence for that until I was writing the 11th chapter in my book. But that finding is important confirmation of what you are about to read.

PART 1:
CHAPTER ONE

THE WHAT, THE HOW, AND THE WHY

Baseball has its secrets. Unlocking them is *the what* of this book. If you like or even love baseball or would just like to learn how to dig deeper into anything you are doing, then you've stepped into the right ballpark. Now there is a price for admission, and that is this: You have to let go of how you see and deal with the obvious. It is a big obstacle.

When we encounter something obvious, we often slide right past it like an unskilled base stealer missing a steal at second base. It is that swoosh, oops, too far, and "You're out!" In this book we will go in and through the obvious in baseball to find things that are not obvious. And amazingly, what we find will in time become obvious as well. They're like lessons or insights taken from baseball itself—*keep your eyes on the ball*—and you can apply those lessons or insights to anything you do in life.

The secrets I am writing about are not the hidden-by-a-glove, change-in-his-grip type of secret that a pitcher conceals before sending a batter that nasty 95 mph curveball. Swing-and-a-miss! Oh yeah. Gotta love that. Rather, this book is about the hidden stuff in baseball that can shed new light on the sport.

Let me call a quick time-out and step into some abstract theory here for just a second. All of us know that the physical world has a structure to it: Things used in baseball such as leather and wood break down into physical structures such as molecules, atoms, and subatomic particles. Most of us know that a baseball is made of leather, string, yarn, rubber, and cork—am I missing anything? But separate from structure, the physical world also has a nature to it— meaning it has both a nature, and, separately, a structure to it. The same holds true of the abstract world. That means there is the physical nature of a bat, a ball, and a base, but there is also the abstract nature of a bat, a ball, and a base. That abstract nature is something entirely different and something we will dive into and discover in this book, shedding new light on the sport itself.

For example, it is the abstract nature of a baseball bat that can help us distinguish between a stick and a baseball bat. That distinction, as you will discover, is critical to baseball's origin history. Also, in baseball there is the physics behind how a 95 mph curveball works. But there is also the abstract nature of the curveball as it is used in a competition, and that abstract nature is what makes the curveball part of a professional sport, and not a children's game. Believe it or not—and it will become obvious—that difference in abstract natures is also key to baseball's history.

The how of this book involves discoveries not just in baseball's physical nature but in its abstract nature.

The stadium-sized lesson, if you will, is this: If the physical world has a nature and a structure to it, shouldn't the abstract world have a nature and a structure to it? Of course it does. Amazingly, it is the abstract world that dictates how the physical world works. This is true of baseball. We can use the abstract nature of it to dig deeper into baseball than ever before and make the sport come to life in a new way.

Do you want to know *the why* of this book? Here is an unfortunate, but good, example:

This quote is taken (retrieved again on May 1, 2023) from a Library of Congress exhibition called "Baseball Americana." It is to the right of an illustration from a children's book first published in 1744. (We will show that illustration in chapter 10 when we go into this in more detail.) For now, let's focus on the accompanying text. Here it is:

"This tiny children's book debunks the great myth that baseball was born in the United States. It is a reprint of John Newbery's work, first published in England in 1744, but it marks the first American reference to baseball in print:"

Let me deconstruct it.

First, think of the words used: "tiny" "debunks" "great" "myth."

If they were truly just trying to be objective, they might have written it something more like this: This children's book is evidence baseball was not born in the United States.

But that is not what you read there, is it? It sounds like another David and Goliath story—not just a tiny book, but a tiny children's book, that smashes down not just a belief, or some history, or some story, but a myth; and it's not just a myth, but a great myth. Wow. And the American myth just comes tumbling down now?

As a side note—and this is strictly my opinion, but you are welcome to share it—the choice of words hints that there is a gleefulness to it when taken as a whole: You silly Americans thought baseball came from the US. Well, it doesn't.

Second, how is a book from 1744 England the "first American reference"? Whatever could that mean?

But there is a deeper problem, and thus there's *the why* of this book: Those two sentences from that Library of Congress exhibit are not even close to the truth. Not even close. We'll get deep into that.

Here's the bigger problem: How is it that so many of those who have played the sport seriously, or even with a measure of passion, or have read stories about its history and great players—naturally, Babe Ruth comes to mind—or have watched a great World Series, are convinced, just know, or deeply feel that baseball was born in America, yet most historians suggest otherwise? I am not writing about emotions here but something deeper—something akin to what some married couples suggest about love at first sight: Intuition. Gut feeling. Are we to assume that intuition counts for absolutely nothing? The experience of countless millions would suggest otherwise.

Let me first stress that researchers are actually great, as are most fans. So, my apology. Again, apology—research is one thing, conclusions are another—but these researchers just happen to be wrong in many of their conclusions. As you will discover, secrets long hidden in baseball strongly suggest that they are in fact *off base*. So why is that? How did this all happen? We will dive into all that.

Lastly, marketing suggests that not everyone is interested in baseball origin history—this book is not just about that, so hang in there. However, in a deeper, more emotional, even patriotic way, many, many Americans emphatically believe that baseball was born of America and that they are linked to it as the American pastime. It is an accepted point of pride that has been pushed back by these historical narratives. In other words, getting to the truth is important.

Hey, we also love football, basketball, and other sports. But as a major sport, American baseball was the first, and it was driven by the culture found in the emerging soul of a nation that would rise to the top of the world. Don't forget that baseball's success paved the way for the other major sports. Those other professional sports are very American, but baseball *is* America.

It's simply time to bring that national pastime on home . . . forever!

CHAPTER TWO

SIMPLE ENOUGH, A
BASEBALL
VERSUS A SOFTBALL

In part I of this book, we are going to walk through part of a concept model on baseball. That means we're going to look at the sport from a new angle—in an even deeper way.

Think of it like letting baseball itself tell us its own story and reveal its deeper and wonderful secrets.

Let's start with this: I am going to ask you to use your imagination. In my right hand, I'm holding up a baseball. In my left hand, I'm holding up a softball. Both kind of cool, right?

Fig. 1

There are three obvious things here, and in keeping with our sports theme, here is my first pitch:

The first thing that is obvious is that the sports are related, right? And if you look at the shape, the stitching, and perhaps the size of each ball—relatively speaking—they look similar. You can see that. It's obvious.

And if you know a little bit about the history, you know that baseball preceded softball as a sport. So right off that bat—*slam!*—you totally know that a softball originated from a baseball. That again is obvious, right?

Well, guess what? I just threw you a curveball. You popped it up—*and you're out!* The true origin of a softball came from something else: a boxing glove. And here's the concept or essence of it:

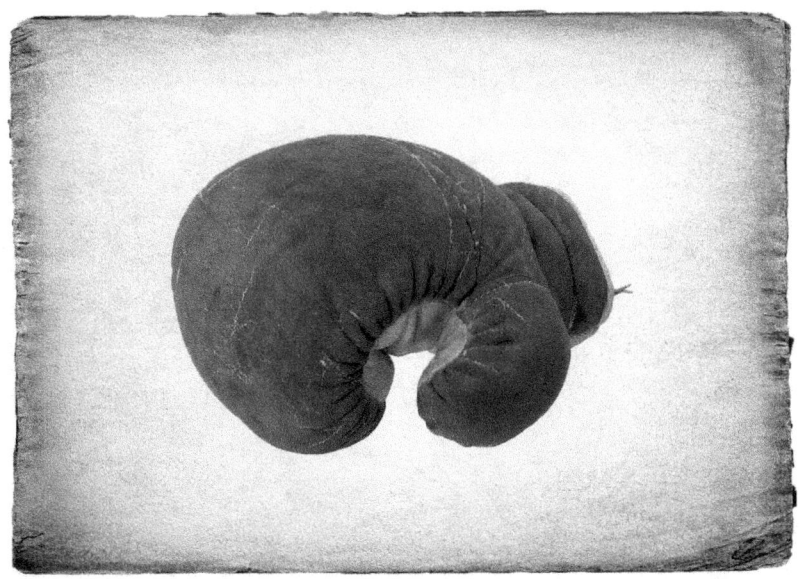

Fig. 2

That soft quality found in a softball came from the texture of a boxing glove, wrapped tightly and into a ball—the approximate size of, you guessed it, a softball. A new sport was launched.

So with that knowledge, when you visualize the softball back in my left hand and now a boxing glove in my right, you can imagine it, or better still, you can almost feel it. In terms of size and texture, a softball truly is more like a boxing glove.

You could feel that if you had one in your hand and you gripped it—that softer feel and obviously that softness inspired the name: Softball! And you wouldn't get there from a baseball alone. And you actually already know why—because a baseball is often called the exact opposite—"Let's play hardball!"

Now that, for me, is kind of cool, so here's my pitch: First, this is a great example of why you need to concept model things first. It's also a great example of what this book is about: The Obvious Isn't.

Even in the simplest of things like a softball—can you get any simpler—there is something obvious and there's something that isn't.

In concept modeling we never take anything—even the most basic of things—for granted. We go into and through the obvious, digging deeper and deeper, until we find and lock down the essence of something; in doing that we often find what isn't obvious—that is, until it too becomes obvious.

CHAPTER THREE
BASEBALL? WHAT'S UP WITH THAT?

We're concept modeling the sport of baseball.

But now I may have a problem with a lot of you readers because I threw that last curveball question at you on the basis of the origin of a softball. It's a problem because the next question is actually even more obvious. And you'd be surprised how many people think I'm trying to trick them by asking this. But let's relax about this. Let's answer the obvious question with an obvious answer.

So what is the one thing you must have to play baseball?

There are many things you need, but this one is at the top of the pyramid: the most important physical thing you need to play baseball.

And, yes, like a fly ball—*slam!*—it pops into your mind almost immediately: A ball.

Most of you are ready to use this highly technical term, and say, "**Duh!**" But hang in there. Stay in our game. It's about to get very interesting.

What is the second most obvious item you need in playing the sport of baseball?

Go back to your sixth grade. School is finished for the day, and you have some extra time before the sun sets. You and your buddies are looking for something fun to do. So you turn to one of them and say something like this: "Hey, Charlie, go get your baseball. I'll go get... a bat."

And that's the answer. Bat!

So now here is where it gets interesting, at least from a concept modeling perspective, because you've got to ask this:

Why isn't it called batball? Baseball? What's up with that? *Base*?

In essence—meaning at its abstract core and defined by the game itself and not by marketing or history—this great sport we all love is actually batball.

Now don't go taking your priceless 1884 Louisville Slugger to me just yet because I am not saying we should change the name. "Baseball" is by far the better name. By far.

But there is something deeper to discover here.

Here is a look at my first crack at doing a concept model on baseball, done in 2008 but included in my 2020 book on concept:

Ball: (The answer to what is the first thing you need?)

Fig. 3: Baseball Concept Model, *Concerning the Nature and Structure of Concept*, by Winston J Perez, 2020, page 182

Bat: (The answer to what is the second thing you need?)

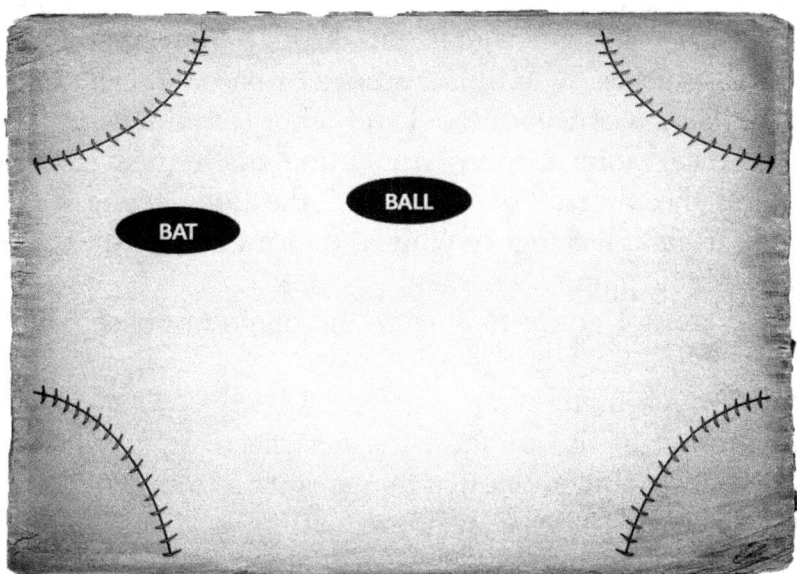

Fig. 4: Baseball Concept Model, *Concerning the Nature and Structure of Concept*, by Winston J Perez, 2020, page 187

So at its core, baseball has physical priorities that are very clear: (1) a ball and (2) a bat.
1. One has to throw a ball toward a player.
2. That player has to hit the ball with a bat.

Then and only then do either bases or gloves come into play. Thus, ball and bat come first. No bat and ball? No baseball. (The model will step into base and glove later.)

Batball Versus Baseball

Probably for some of you, that wasn't obvious, but now, suddenly, it is. Others reading this may remain skeptical—all good. No issue with that at all. But more likely, for most of you reading this, it may have been something you just never thought about. "Baseball?" Where does that come from? *Base*? That is a fascinating question—and we will be concept modeling that soon because the answer to that helps prove baseball comes from the United States.

As you read the paragraphs above, you were stepping directly into concept modeling through the actual creation of a concept model on baseball. (Obviously, there is much more to the model.) Think of it like discovering a "fossil" from a dinosaur—something you can then use to guide, and more importantly, to interpret your research. Only this time that animal is baseball, and our focus is not just the physical, but the abstract. We go in and through the physical to reach the abstract—which is where the essence of baseball can be found. We dial it in using a concept model and other techniques.

One technical note: Concept modeling distinguishes between "batball" and the phrase "bat-and-ball," the latter being a generic phrase often used as a category while the former may be used as the name for a specific game.

But if we are not going to change the name of "baseball," why does it matter?

It matters in research.

As mentioned in the preface, the abstract world is hidden in physical baseball, which includes things such as a bat, ball, or base and physical activities such as running, batting, and base stealing. In that abstract world, things are defined not just by the physical but by essence. Without that part of reality, a bat is just a polished stick.

During an afternoon practice, one can throw an easy ball toward a batter—make it hittable—and call it pitching, but that is an entirely different animal than what we find in a competitive game at a major league ballpark. One is not the same as the other despite the fact that we may call it by the same word: a pitch. It is the reason why major league pitching at its core is defined by the nature of baseball's competitive battle. Obvious, right? But, as we will see, the nature of that competition alone changes what we understand, or even define, as baseball's origin history.

The abstract world of baseball has a nature and structure that is hidden. It is the abstract side at the heart of baseball that reveals the deeper truth about it, which we are rolling out within this book. Again, it is the abstract world that dictates how the physical world functions. Accordingly, if it matters how you define things such as a bat, a baseball (not just any ball), a base, a pitch, or even batting, then it matters how you define the sport and where it truly originated.

One note: If all this abstract world stuff matters in baseball, then it matters in everything—period.

And finally, think of the name *baseball* from the bat's perspective. If we could interview Mr. Bat himself, he might slam it out, "I want to know why it isn't called batball!"

Mr. Bat might then make his case, "Baseball? Base? Why not batball? I mean I do half the work, you know! I am in on every play, every pitch, every inning! I get picked up and swung around all the time. I smack the ball when I can! And I make home runs possible!

"Base? He don't do nothin'! He just sits there! Ain't nobody going to take him home or give him a brand name, like a Louisville Slugger! All the base does is sit there, some ninety feet away. Ninety feet away from home plate. Doing nothing!"

It's true, from the bat's perspective, that is an interesting point. The other aspect is base. Where does that come from? I am going to get to that in detail in part II and III, when we do concept modeling on the origin history of baseball because that's where I think a lot of people are *off base*. (Pun accidental again, but immediately claimed as intentional!)

But for now, you should consider that it probably comes from two things: A time when bases were actually more important than bats. Hard to believe but true. And one game that preceded baseball that many researchers and historians tend to undervalue. I will cover that game in chapter nineteen.

Next, we're going to take a deeper concept modeling step into baseball and define the attributes of a baseball with some added fun.

CHAPTER FOUR

ATTRIBUTES. AND BRADY'S HOME TEAM ADVANTAGE

It's kind of fascinating in a way. You already know the answers to these next questions. You already know what the attributes of a baseball are. But change your thinking. Be open. We just don't think this way that often. We just don't think deeply about the things right in front of us. We assume we know them—"Of course, I know what a ball is"—and then we throw them into the *it's obvious* bucket.

Well the truth is that you know at least the first three. But there is a fourth one. And that one is literally *hard* to spot. So when you look at a baseball and see it as a physical thing, what is the most obvious characteristic? What is the most basic attribute it has?

One, a baseball is round.

It's so obvious that it's *hard* to see—to recognize instantly when asked about it. Amazingly, our minds are not trained to stop and stick to the obvious. When it's too obvious, we hesitate—not everyone and not every time—but it is something to note in how we really look at the world. A football is not round. A baseball is. It is that simple too. It is so obvious that we skip right by it.

Round is almost the first thing you have to say about a baseball. It is an attribute. There's more to explore there coming up, but I want to skip to the second attribute, which is also very evident. You notice that a baseball is not just round; it is leather. Right? Leather is a second attribute on our list or lineup.

The third attribute is—can you think of it? We have round; we have leather. The next attribute, giving you time to guess, is this: A baseball is small. That is the third attribute in our lineup.

But the word *small* is a relative term, right? For example, we introduced this book looking at a small baseball versus a bigger softball. But compared to a basketball, they are both pretty small.

Did you ever consider the fact that there's only one size for a baseball, yet there are three sizes for a softball: eleven inches, twelve inches, and sixteen inches.

Here's a side note: The sixteen-inch size is used for what they call Chicago-style softball, where they sometimes use no gloves. How fun is that? Because Chicago still loves the sport that was launched at the Farragut Boat Club in Chicago.

Baseballs are always the same size. Do you want to know what that size is? Here's the deeper truth: A baseball is the perfect size. And that is true. That is a correct answer!

Even more amazing, baseball got to that perfect size—what I would call in concept modeling "the perfected size"—without the aid of science. In fact, relatively speaking, science has only recently discovered and proved that a baseball is indeed the perfect size.

But now, I want to talk Tom Brady stuff. Something he personally might find interesting, or not. For attributes, we have round, leather, small. And one more which we will get to. Those four attributes together are the basis for the term home-field advantage.

You see, in the early days, as baseball grew in popularity and teams were created, it was always the home team that provided the football, I mean the baseball. This meant that they could make their baseballs bigger, smaller, smoother not-so-smooth, or even softer—any way they wanted to.

And so if another team was coming to town, they might not be used to a little different feel for the ball, well maybe it was a little bit squishier or a bit—I guess you could call it—deflated! That would definitely give the team providing that squishy ball a distinct, slight "home-team advantage." You know, kind of deflating the visiting team's hopes a bit?

Since the home team was used to their own feel, that would, even if only psychologically, give the home team a home-team advantage. You know, I guess you could say that really was the American way—they were all Patriots! Kind of makes everything better, doesn't it? Definitely.

Of course, though true, we are having some dugout fun here. I like and admire Tom Brady (truly the GOAT), not as a team fan, but for his work ethic—which can lead you or anyone to success. And to be candid, really folks? These guys are paid millions. They are top athletes, and we're wasting ink on Deflategate? In baseball, if you make changes to a ball, it's a huge deal. That's not true in football.

Why not treat it like the early days. Visiting teams would just say, "You wait! We'll get ya! Oh yeah. We will!" And folks, all that silliness is like saying no home team crowd should be allowed to make any noise whatsoever, since it creates a real home team advantage. A warning was all that was needed, something like this:

"Grow the you-know-what up!"

All that aside, in fact, all that ball sizing was important—in fact, very important! Small as an attribute of a baseball's size was being worked out by trial and error. Different sizes were everywhere, yet all of them eventually were heading to one and only one size—a baseball as a baseball is today.

Concept modeling suggests everything has a tendency to work toward something "perfected." And baseball is no different. In other words, when it comes to the concept of small, a baseball was always headed toward a very specific size, no matter what.

That size, that perfected size, is the size of the palm of a man's hand. And that matters. And you probably have guessed why. It was always headed to the perfect size for pitching, and the pitcher and batter duel. It's not the word small that matters; it's the concept or essence of that word in relationship to the sport of baseball.

Think of this: Major League Baseball has six pages describing how a professional baseball must be made in order to be official.

Now, all of us have had those wonderful eureka moments. Even mini-eureka waves coming at us feel great. Well, let's see if we can generate one—get it coming toward us—closer and closer right now.

We have one, two, three important aspects—round, leather, and small—as attributes. Now, can you think of the fourth? And this is the tricky one. What is the fourth attribute of a baseball? If you were to have a baseball in front of you, what is the one characteristic besides those three that you would notice about it.

You could roll it around in your hands, you could feel the leather, you could check out the size, but there's one more characteristic coming out of that experience. Can you guess what that is? By the way, I kind of slid it past you a few times.

That's the idea that a baseball is hard.

Now, when you concept model anything, you have to be open to what your intuition may start to whisper to you or at times even shout at you. I love it because the word hard is not so obvious until it is.

And at that very moment, when I was first doing my concept model on baseball almost fourteen years ago, I felt something. I felt the beginning of a eureka wave headed in my direction.

So stop. See if you can feel it—a wave coming and headed toward your mind. I don't know if it is, and this is not some foo-foo stuff. It's just that for some of you reading this for the first time, the word *hard* seems to have something deeper about it, as it applies to baseball.

Hard! Is there something deeper there? Absolutely.

By the way, email me at info@conceptmodeling.com if you experience a bit of what I'm talking about right now. If you have that feeling. I'd be curious. (I'll send you the results of the poll.)

In this case, my intuition suggested to me that there was something unique about that word. So in my concept model presentation, I actually separated it out—and that was before I understood what made that attribute so unique.

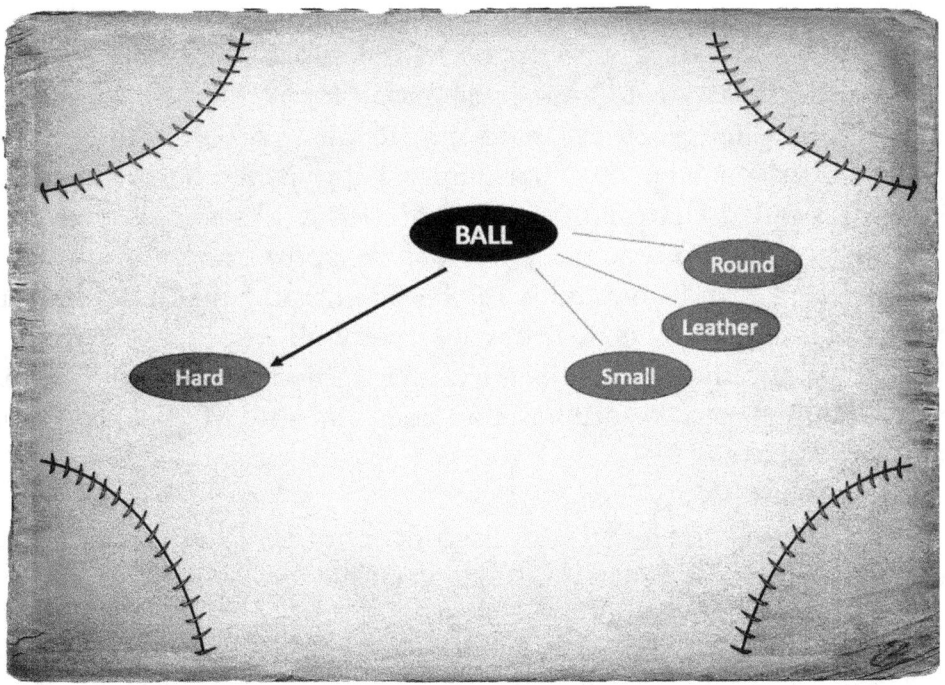

Fig. 5 Taken from *Concerning the Nature and Structure of Concept*, by Winston J Perez, 2020 and the baseball concept model done in 2008

First, is the fact that *hard*, as a term, kind of captures the other attributes and kind of glues them altogether into perfection. Like with the physical baseball itself, it's the thing that stitches it all together.

Second, the word hard is a unique concept when applied to baseball. Why? Because a baseball is not really hard, yet it is! I love that apparent contradiction. That's because it's more of a quality—that hard-not-hard quality is unique to a baseball.

This is one of those *The Obvious Isn't* things because you could call it hard, but at the same time this leather-texture-feel makes it slightly less than hard.

The Obvious Isn't...in Baseball

To illustrate the point, what if the baseball were actually a golf ball made into the size of a baseball. That would really be a hard ball. And you'd know it because you'd have players breaking way more bats, breaking their shins and arms, even their elbows, wide open. It would have infielders breaking their hands trying to slow a ground ball. And occasionally, players would be just knocked out completely, if not almost killed, by a ball being thrown or hit at them. It would just not be possible to play the sport safely with a baseball-sized golf ball.

So that's obvious. Then why do I still use the word hard? That's the amazing thing I didn't see. I just took it for granted till I connected the dots. This quality of hard, particular to a baseball, is more likely the reason why the "hardball" synonym for baseball stuck: Baseball is called "hardball" and it works. It works so well that, like softball, *hardball* could actually work as the sport's name.

For the record, I love the name baseball, and I like it better. But that's not the point. This is: The word "hardball" captures the round, the leather, and the small—the attributes unified into a whole—even better than the actual word baseball does. I'm sure Mr. Bat would be happy to hear that.

Mr. Bat might say, *"Oh yeah!"*

And there is an element to the concept of *hard* that is unique to the sport—it's so cool that almost every player loves to say, "Hey, let's play some hardball!"

It's not too hard, thus safe, so you can handle it. You kind of sense that. Like James Bond, we all want to be *tough*—but only up to a point. Up to the point that we can personally handle. A baseball is as hard as it can be without being too dangerous.

That hardness quality is impacted not only by the round and the small, but also obviously because it's made of leather. *Hard* is what makes the pitcher-and-batter duel, at the heart of the game, possible. We're talking about the curveball and the home run, just to name two.

And if you're in a baseball park and there's a fly ball headed your way, you can actually attempt to catch it with your bare hands. It might sting a little, but you'll survive. And boy, isn't that worth the price of admission? And isn't that another reason people love to go to the ballpark—hoping to catch a fly ball someday?

So when you look at the core elements of baseball as a sport, *hard* is actually there at the core. And to me that was the eureka moment. It's called hardball, and it has stuck for a reason, not just as a side note—not as just a throwaway term. That is cool.

And did you catch it? *Slam*, right into your mitt! It's amazing. It is unexpected; there are a few other sports where you have a nickname. What's a nickname for football, for hockey, for soccer? Anyone? Anyone?

Yeah, a couple of you might be thinking b-ball, but that is an abbreviation—there is no such thing as f-ball, s-ball, h-ball, or the like.

And it just might be that baseball started the whole nickname thing in sports. Did you know that "Giants" and "Pirates" were actually nicknames first—before they became official team names? And who doesn't remember this guy's nick name? The Babe!

And hard means more than just saying this ball is soft or hard. You don't do that in football. Mr. Brady would never say this football is too hard, would he? Oops.

Don't think of the word *hard* as a word. Think of it as a concept. And that's the difference.

So finally, in terms of the development of baseball as a sport, *round* alone doesn't do it. *Leather*—you know a football is leather too—doesn't do it. And *small* doesn't do it. *Hard* unifies those. A baseball had to work as something you could pitch, hit, and catch!

So, I think I have squeezed that one attribute as much as I can. But that is also the lesson: how deep the simplest of things in reality go.

Foul Ball

Now, a few of you may be feeling a little perturbed right now, and you would be right to feel that way. What about the stitching on a baseball? Clearly that is an attribute of a baseball, so there should be five attributes—round, leather, small, hard—plus stitching. Fun fact: Those red stitches—108 of them—are all double stitches.

In fact, a brilliant colleague named Larry who is far smarter than I am pointed it out to me after the first edition of this book. Of course stitching is an attribute. I love that because, well, it kind of proves that the obvious isn't. Even a guy trained to look for the obvious missed it. Lesson learned. Almost.

You see, I went back to my original notes. I had done the concept model back in 2008, and I am so attached to it because it introduced me to yet a deeper layer of structure within the abstract world, which we will cover throughout this book. In other words, the model I did in 2008 (one of the first graphically designed concept models I ever did) is what makes this book possible. So here are two lessons:

First, I am attached to that first model. I don't want to change it. That is a big lesson, and I will talk about our unconscious agendas and our egos throughout this book. In fact, how about we do some of that right now? Yes, perhaps my ego was getting in the way. That is what happens. We see things as obvious, and our ego throws any deeper consideration away. Of course I know what a frigging baseball is, right?

Second, there is a historical twist here. You see, when I went back to review my concept modeling back in 2008, I also remember having this debate: Is stitching a primary attribute or a subattribute of a ball? In other words, is stitching a subattribute of *leather* as seen below? And that is a fascinating question. At least to me as a concept modeling guy, it's fascinating because discovering and breaking down those distinctions is key to locking down the essence of something. Not what we think something is, but what it really is.

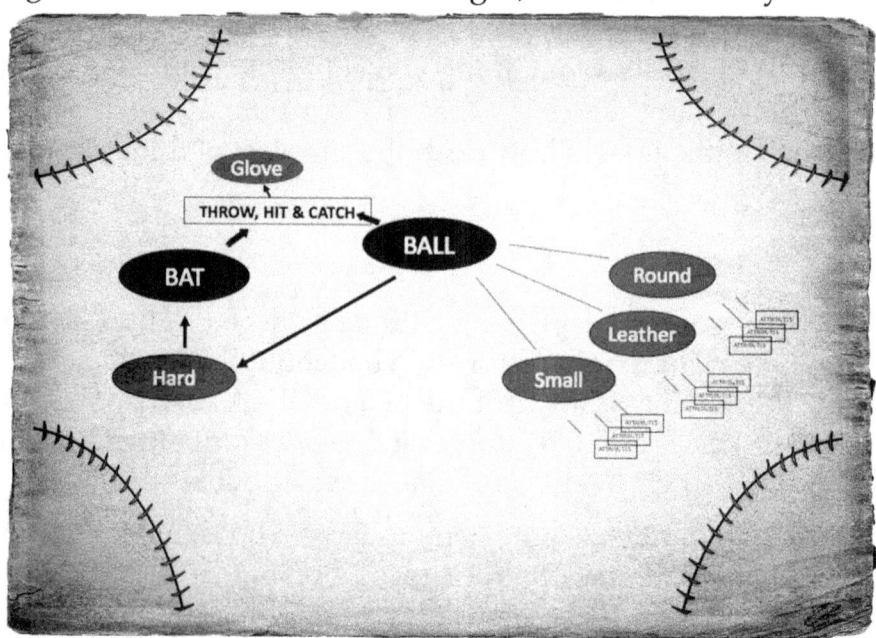

Fig. 6 Leather & Attributes—Baseball Concept Model, by Winston J Perez, 2008

I am not sure I was thinking about a baseball today, but a baseball as it was in its beginning—meaning at a time when there were no curve balls, knuckle balls, sliders, and the like, and the stitching was not red. It was just there to hold the leather together. No leather. No stitching. And that is important to concept modeling. Order and priorities are important. The amazing thing is that priorities can shift over time, and that is also important—innovations stem from that. So I updated the model to reflect that along with other elements:

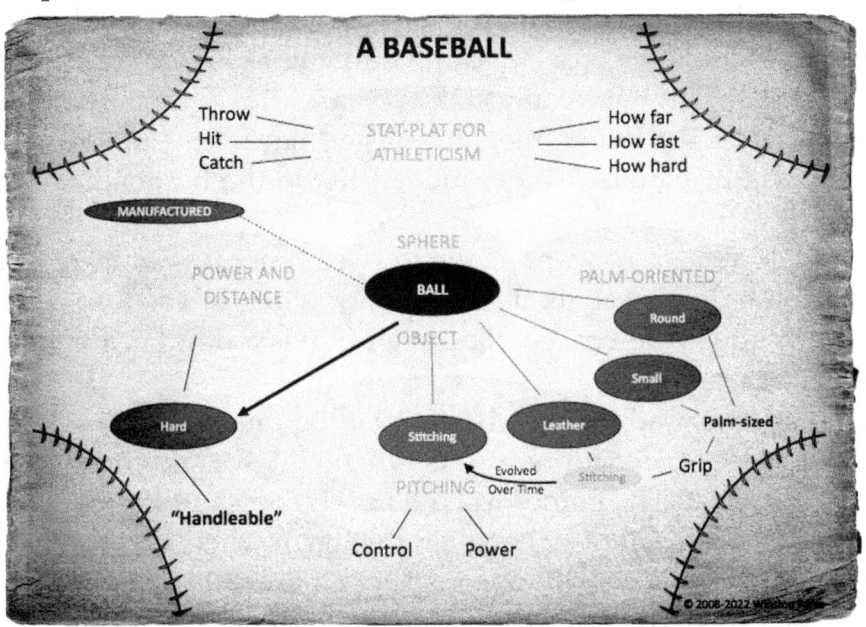

Fig. 7 Updated (2022) Baseball (Ball) Concept Model, by Winston J Perez

And at that moment, it dawned on me: This—baseball stitching in the early days of the game—is what I call a "shadow concept." Inside the core bundle of concepts of something is often a single element or concept that is less noticeable; it is present but barely visible, much like a shadow. These are things that, presently, are of less importance within the core of something; but given time, they may emerge as significant or even game changing in the future. The stitching of a baseball is exactly that: A shadow concept. (Shadow concepts are further explained in my book Concerning the Nature and Structure of Concept).

The cigarette lighter in your car is a great example. It was not designed to do anything but light a cigarette in the beginning. But inherent inside the concept was what fire was to cavemen: energy. Today, it can be used to energize your smart phone, your computer, or anything you want to plug directly into the socket—and it won't burn it to ashes. That's amazing.

Early on, the stitching on a baseball was just holding the leather together. It was not as distinct or functional as it is today. Of course, back then, you could see it and feel it, but it really was all about the leather. It was all about the cover of a ball. Compared to today, it was definitely in the shadows. And the hint is that it was not till the 1900s that color stitches on a baseball came into vogue. As we will see, it is no coincidence that it was only sixteen years after overhand pitching was allowed in the game, meaning faster, harder-to-spot baseballs were coming at batters. Colors indeed made the baseball easier to spot quickly.

So stitching as a concept changed over time. It is indeed now a core attribute of a baseball, but it was not when it was first used. It was not obvious when baseball began, but it is today. How cool. The obvious truly isn't.

(Note: If you read the word "stat-plat" in the model, that term is actually a place holder for now. It is functional, so it might stick. The concept is correct. The name? Maybe not. It comes from my concept modeling of a *base* and I will explain that term when we deconstruct a *base*—that's right, we will deconstruct a baseball *base*. Amazingly, there is a lot to learn that is hidden in baseball.)

(Graphic note: Some of the lettering within our graphs are lighter in color. That is by design to indicate that those concepts reside in a deeper layer of our concept model. Concepts are always layered.)

In the next chapter, or inning, we will go into a totally different characteristic concerning the nature of baseball.

CHAPTER FIVE

RELATIONSHIPS AND YES, DISRUPTIVE TECHNOLOGY
IN BASEBALL

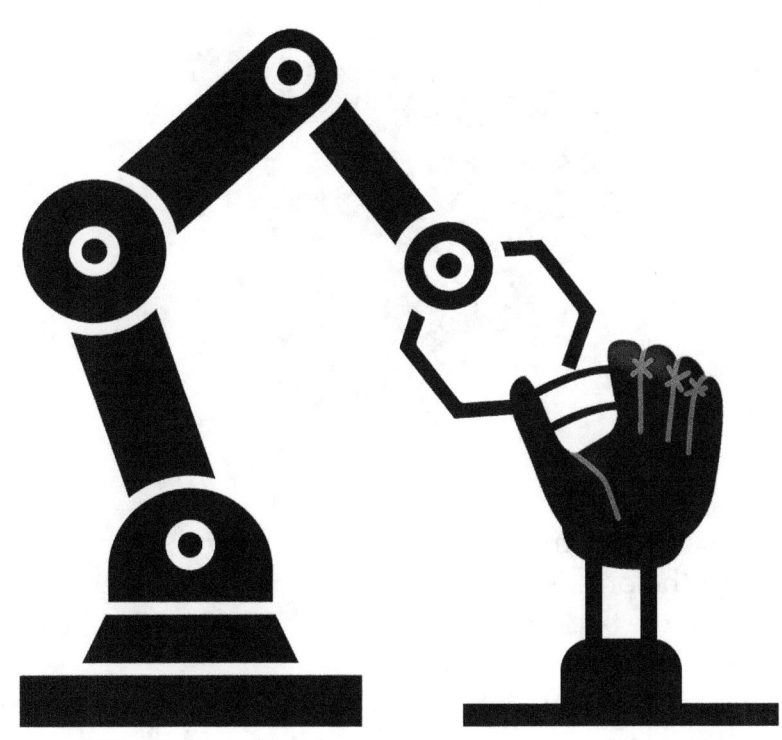

We're deconstructing baseball. Now we're going to talk about relationships. And again, in this chapter, I'm going to start out with things that are simple. Obvious. But this time I want to show you the value of doing that in your own profession. And one of the best examples is going to be what I call *baseball string theory*—literally disruptive technology. Can disruptive technology apply to baseball? Absolutely.

In fact, in the stadium of your mind, you can almost hear this: A vendor in the aisle shouting out, "Popcorn, peanuts, disruptive technology. Popcorn, peanuts, disruptive technology!"

Deconstructing the Abstract

When I say deconstruction, I am talking about it from a concept modeling point of view. In other words, I am not just talking about the physical, but the abstract.

Let me give you a simple example:

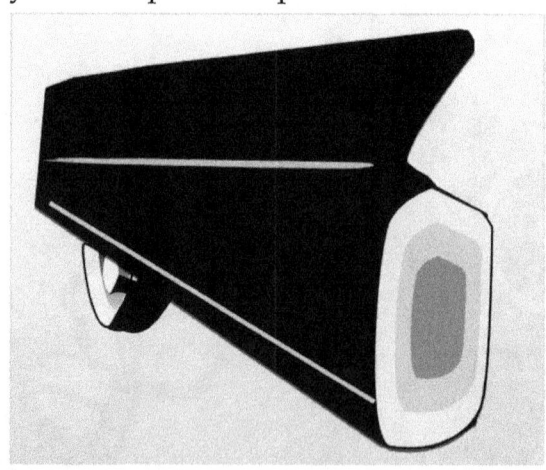

(Fig. 8)

In the seventies my brother was given a 1963 black Cadillac. Those were the ones that looked like Batmobiles with the fins that projected out the back. How cool were they? Very. But he decided to deconstruct the car and rebuild it.

I read somewhere that the average number of parts in a car is thirty thousand. So you can imagine what it looked like when I walked into a two-door garage, back home, and saw probably ten thousand parts spread across the garage floor.

When we think about deconstruction, we usually think physical:

You take the parts apart, put them on the floor, and later, after cleaning them or whatever, you put them back together. So simple. But that leaves out the abstract elements.

When you talk about a car, you are talking about the abstract concept of *transportation* or the activity of *racing* or *driving*. Right? In concept modeling, we actually focus on those abstract elements. The deconstruction of physical things is just a way to get down deeper into the concept elements because when those concepts shift, as we're going to see, everything shifts. Innovations are born.

We've also just seen an example of this because in baseball we started with the physical things of a bat and a ball. Now we're going to step into some relationships—or abstract things.

So in my model, in between the words "ball" and "bat," I have a box, and in that box are three words: throw, hit, and catch. (See Fig. 6) Can any three words be simpler? And I know some of you may be thinking well that's "toooo obvious." But change your thinking.

First of all, as an example, all of the most sophisticated computer programs that track weather, drive communications, and launch rockets all come down to zeros and ones. In baseball, that zero and that one is a baseball and a bat. From those two stem all activities. From the zeros and ones in computers you get the activity of showing you directions while you're driving in your car in real time.

But then there's something else: All those activities I just mentioned, all three, are elevated into specialized athletic skills that become almost art forms, as you'll see when we talk about pitching.

Now, if art forms are not enough for you, don't turn you on, then think finances. Because players who become great at those skills—because those skills are so highly valued—get paid well. And as we all know, many become millionaires. So, fortune is part of the equation.

Another part of the equation is fame. One of the better examples is the Wheaties box. So let me tell you a side note: In 1934 the very first athlete was placed on a Wheaties box, and his name was Lou Gehrig. So here's the key: from the simplicity of relationships come skills that will make players famous and wealthy.

So in my concept model, there is a box—throw, hit, catch—and leading from that box is a line going to a circle with one word in it: glove (See Fig. 6).

Amazingly, we've gone from two physical things, a bat and a ball, to activities and then back to a physical thing. There may be some of you who are thinking, well, that's the core of baseball: A bat, a ball, and a glove. That is true today. But it was not true at the beginning of the sport.

It took twenty-four years, from the very first baseball game, in 1846 (some say 1845), to 1870, when they took a little step toward having a glove in baseball. That came from a catcher who got injured, so that catcher used buckskin to create a mitt and protect his hand while he was catching.

We don't think about it, but imagine how many times a catcher got injured back then, even when the pitching was underhand. Actually, it was pretty difficult for them to last the entire season without any injuries of any kind considering, and I am not sure of this fact, that some of the top teams played over fifty games a year. Try catching a ball without a mitt for fifty games—not that easy to do.

That was 1870. Five years later, in 1875, the first "official" mitt entered the game through Charlie Waitt, who was a St. Louis player. I don't know what it is about St. Louis, but, you see part of the heart of baseball, coming from St Louis. Kind of interesting.

I'll say one thing about Charles. He had to have a little bit of courage because they called him all sorts of names for being like a wimp for using a glove. Can you imagine baseball being played without gloves today? I don't think I can.

Now the fascinating thing is that it took seventy-four years for the very first modern-day baseball glove to come around.

So, now when I get into my *baseball string theory*, there's the importance of the invention of the modern-day glove, which is based on disruptive technology. Do you think that baseball might have had disruptive technology? Absolutely! This is a fantastic example. So, I want to do a shout-out to Chris Silva[3] , who wrote a fascinating article about the history of baseball and the glove.

In his article, he mentions that in 1919 (others mention 1920), a Bill Doak went to the Rawlings Sporting Goods Company with a new innovation in a baseball glove. That innovation involved, you guessed it, two-strings. That simple—going from the thumb to the index finger.

So, now I want you to look at it from a concept modeling point of view or a concept point of view. That was an entire shift in the essence or the nature of what a glove was—going from *protection* to *augmentation*. It was about enhancing the human hand the way computers enhance or augment our ability to process and store information.

From that moment on, a new concept entered into a glove, and that's called the glove's pocket, or technically, the web. So imagine how good it feels today when a ball is hit so hard, and it slams into the web of your glove. No pain but a lot of gain. And we love that.

So, in terms of this book, when we talk about *the obvious isn't*, this is one of the best examples. It is not obvious that two strings could transform a product the way they did.

I harbor a lot of fascination around this string theory for baseball because it's not about baseball. It's about a lesson and a skill you can take into your profession tomorrow! A skill you can take into your creation of new technology or a product today! Or you can take into your creative endeavors. It is the idea that simple physical things can transform not just the external but also the core concept underneath something. We should look out for that.

Hopefully, when I write a book specifically on concept modeling technology, we're going to dive into that because it leads to how we can develop disruptive technology. But for now, learn that the deconstruction of not only physical things but conceptual things can lead to innovations. Why is that important? It's important to your pocketbook because Bill Doak was earning about $25,000 annually in royalties as late as the nineteen fifties. So imagine what that might have meant in real dollars-and-cents value at that time. What do I say about all that? Concept matters.

So, next, in my concept model I have that box of *throw, hit,* and *catch*. And I have a line leading to another box. In that box are two words: *run and score*. Actually, it is three words if you count the "and." (Note: It is not shown in Fig. 6.)

But I want to look at the concept of *run*. Besides pitching and batting, baseball has a specialized skill that we take for granted—until we don't. And some fans have never taken it for granted, and Hall of Fame careers have been driven by this skill. And yet again from a concept modeling point of view, it's one of those *The Obvious Isn't* things.

This skill involves marrying an object to an activity. Do you remember when we were looking at a Cadillac being broken down or disassembled? That's all physical. You break down the physical things, and you put the physical things back together.

How about the marriage of a physical thing with an activity? From a concept modeling point of view, that becomes interesting. All sports do this. But baseball has one specific skill or activity that is unique to baseball. It has made heroes. It has made Hall of Fame players. And that skill, you probably are guessing it, is called base running.

Those simple two things glued together—a base and running—created base stealers. We don't normally think of it this way, but you cannot pick up or touch a "running." You can only touch a physical thing that is running.

And if you were great at base stealing, you not only became wealthy; you probably landed in the Hall of Fame.

I want to write about four of those players.

His nick-name was Sliding Billy. His real name was Billy (William) Hamilton who played between the years of 1888 and 1901. Currently, he is number three on the list of all-time base stealers. That is because he had stolen 914 bases. That's kind of cool. Listed as the number two of all time in base stealing is a name you'll recognize: Lou Brock. Lou passed away while I was working on this podcast and book, so our thoughts and prayers go out to him and his family. He was great.

How important is base stealing to baseball? In 1974, Lou came in second in ballot voting for the MVP for the National League. The reason? He had stolen 118 bases, which was the single-season record for most stolen bases up to that time. The excitement of seeing these guys closing in on stealing a base is one of the great things in baseball.

Now, at number one on the list, and by far, is Rickey Henderson, who stole 1,406 bases in his twenty-four-year career.

Let me tell you a side note: His parents obviously loved musicians and music because part of Rickey's real name is Rickey Nelson. Yes, his parents named him after Ricky Nelson the singer, so that's kind of fun. The second thing, which is even more fun, is that Rickey was born in the back of an Oldsmobile on its way to the hospital.

Later he would joke about it, saying, "I was always fast! I couldn't wait." Now that is a fast guy!

But do you remember the excitement of watching him when he got on first base? Everybody in the stadium knew what he was going to do. The other team knew what he was going to do, and yet, sure enough, he still accomplished it. That's pretty amazing.

The fourth guy on the list I saved because he is considered one of the greatest players of all time. In fact, *The Sporting News* puts him at number three on their "Baseball's 100 Greatest Players" list. His name? Ty Cobb.

I am going to jump back to Lou Brock for a second because it was in 1977 at Jack Murphy Stadium in San Diego that Brock beat the record that was established by Ty Cobb for most stolen bases. That number was 892. Ty Cobb was one of the early players who defined the skills needed to play the sport of baseball. Part of that was stealing bases or using his skill as a base runner. Kind of cool!

In the next chapter, we are going to look at one of the deepest layers, or hidden concept, underneath baseball. More specifically, this was something that was still somewhat hidden back when I did the model in 2008. Today, the existence of that concept is now common knowledge yet the subject of debate. It is what has fueled the controversial rise in what they call analytics. But all of that is only possible because of this concept—something that was always there yet never tapped into.

CHAPTER SIX

THE ONCE HIDDEN CONCEPT AT THE CORE BASEBALL

The Obvious Isn't...in Baseball

We've come to the inning, so to speak, that changes the entire game. It actually separates baseball from every other sport, and the reason for that is not obvious—at least it was not until relatively recently. In fact, it is still a bit hard to believe because all sports now involve this concept—just not like baseball.

This section is the reverse of the title because at one time this was truly not obvious. Given the changes in how many professional teams are currently managed, it has been made pretty clear in recent years.

When I say *the obvious isn't,* I mean it both ways: Some things are obvious and some things are not. Yet given time and development, it all becomes obvious. That concept in baseball? *Numbers.*

"Numbers" is the core concept that underlies all of baseball in every respect. For that reason, using concept modeling terms, that concept is what I call a transcept—meaning something that transcends all of the other concepts at the core of something; in this instance, baseball. And again, the something that influences all other baseball-related concepts is *numbers.*

Even if you've heard it, let it sink in anew: *numbers*. But don't confuse numbers with just analytics or post-game analysis.

And, yes, it is that simple. But it's also deep. Very deep. Now for many of you reading this, you already sense that. It has been written or talked about a lot nowadays. But for most of baseball history it was not that obvious. Some say it came to shining light during the amazing 2002 run by the Oakland Athletics, and more recently, with the Tampa Bay Rays in 2020. More importantly, what you may not know is how deep, deep, and deeper that concept goes in baseball.

Again, by numbers, I don't mean stats either—or I should say—I don't mean just stats. Stats are part of it, but only a part of it. They are just one manifestation of how "numbers" bubble up from the bottom and impact every aspect of the game.

Still, you may want to point to the obvious: Don't other sports have stats?

Not like baseball.

Or maybe you're thinking, well, other sports involve numbers. For example, football. Football has a hundred-yard-long field between the goal lines. It has fifty-three and a third yard-wide field; it has four quarters; it has six points for a touchdown and one for an extra point.

And basketball —what about that? It has a set court size of ninety-four feet by fifty feet and rims that are ten feet high. Don't other sports involve numbers in some way?

Not like baseball.

And what about this? Don't other sports have scoring?

Not like baseball.

So count 'em: Those are three strikes, and instead of going against baseball, they might be going against me. Some of you may want to be calling me out before I have even gotten up to bat: "Winston— *you're outta here!*"

Well let's see if I can make a game out of it. For the rest of this inning (chapter) it's all going to be about how the concept of numbers is tightly woven into the essence of baseball.

Where do I start? Why not with our concept model? Remember, we talked about relationships, right? *Throw, hit, catch*. But we've already talked about catch and the glove. Now it's time to get to the core of the sport, which is: *Throw-hit*. That combination is the essence of the sport—the pitcher-versus-batter duel.

So, let's talk about the pitching mound. The pitching mound, or actually the rubber, is sixty feet, six inches from home plate. It has stuck to that distance for well over a hundred years (since 1893) for a reason. Today, if the pitching mound was five feet closer, the pitcher would get the advantage. By the way, at one time it was.

It is a little complicated because a number of things were going on. That's because, in the 1800s, pitching was shifting from underhand to overhand. We forget that. It was literally going from underhand, to sidearm, to overhand. It was also transitioning from a pitcher running and throwing the ball from a large box or area to a pitcher standing in one place, where he used a rubber. When all the different ways and calculations were done, the pitcher was in fact four feet, three and a half inches closer to home plate than today. But keep in mind that, at that time, the pitching was underhand.

Today, if the pitcher was pushed farther back, say five feet farther, the batter would get the advantage. That is the amazing thing: Baseball got to that perfected distance without science. It's only relatively recently that science looked into the numbers in baseball and came out shocked at how precise the numbers in baseball are—they are almost perfect.

Another example is the distance between home plate and first. It's ninety feet. Amazingly, that distance is also perfect. Where would baseball be without the split-second timing involved in a double play? That precise distance makes it a regular feature of the game—not too often and not too rare. It actually makes the double play exciting.

Let me show you some other numbers: This time with pitching. Here, we really get into it. As you know, pitching is truly an art form, and it's extraordinarily so. It is amazing and actually beautiful to watch, but it's made possible by numbers.

So here are just some of those numbers

9 to 9.25
5 to 5.75
7.6
108
5, 4, 3, and 2
1
1
6

Let's go through those:
9 to 9.25—the approximate circumference of a baseball—in inches. It must not be less than 9 or greater than 9.25. There is a reason for that.
5 to 5.75—the weight of a baseball, in ounces. It must not be less than 5 ounces or more than 5.75 ounces.
7.6—the average hand length in inches, stretching from the fingertips to just below the edge of the palm, where you will find the crease.
108 (I love this one)—the number of red double stitches on a baseball; even the height of them can impact a curveball.
4, 3, 2, and 5—numbers related to various pitches. Let's go through them:

- There is a four-seam fastball.
- There is three-finger change up.

- There is the two-finger fastball. (Well, it's not exactly just two.)
- But then there's the circle changeup, in which you hold or position your hand as if you are saying OK to the ball—five fingers are involved with that one.

1—one knee must go up as the body rotates for the windup.
1—one back; one arm must lurch backward then power forward
6—six pages. As mentioned, if you look up the rules on how to make an official baseball, it stretches to six pages. Pretty amazing.

For comparison, how about these numbers:
10 and 18
If you're thinking about other sports, I am going to throw in those numbers. Those are numbers in basketball.
10—10 feet. The height of a basketball rim.
18—18 inches. The width of a basketball rim.

So, in baseball, seventeen inches is the width of home plate. But there are other numbers impacting what you know as the strike zone, and you already know this. The distance from the knees to the player's armpits, basically, impacts the strike zone. (Technically a few inches below.) Can you imagine if the rim in basketball suddenly changed its height, depending on the height of the player? You'd never see that!

Or can you imagine if football players were only allowed to catch a ball if it hit them between their arm pits and their knees? No, you can't imagine that either!

Also, I didn't know this—so I have my doubts—but it appears from data that before some new rules were implemented, the strike zone was actually proven to shrink depending on the count—like a 3-0 versus an 0-2 count. And have any of you ever seen a rim shrink? I didn't think so.

Now, here are the numbers related to the timing within the pitcher and batter duel.

And for this, I want to do a shout-out to Dr. Cynthia Bir[4]., (Her work is referenced in an article, ***"The Science Behind Baseball," Sci-Journer, March 2, 2012***). At this writing, Dr. Cynthia is a Professor and Chair in the Department of Biomedical Engineering at Wayne State University.

The following represent the execution of a pitch and hit, or what I might call a home run swing. Here are those numbers:

90
.4
.10
12
48.5
.07
10
38.5
8.5 to 13.5
30 to 25
.17

Let's go through them:
90—the speed of a 90-mile-an-hour fastball that we're going to use for the next calculations.
.4—the time in seconds that a pitch going at that speed takes to reach the plate. That's four-tenths of a second!
.10—the time, only one-tenth of a second, it takes a batter to actually see or locate the ball.
12—the number of feet the baseball has traveled in that time.
48.5—how many feet the ball has left to travel.
.07—the number of seconds it takes for a player to calculate the speed, angle, and trajectory of the ball. That's seven hundredths of a second!
10—the number of feet the ball has traveled by that time.
38.5—the number of feet that are left for the ball to travel before it goes across home plate.
8.5 to 13.5—the number of feet the ball will travel before the batter must decide on his swing.
30 to 25—the number of feet left to the plate that the ball must travel once the batter has made his decision to swing or not.
.17—the amazing number—let me write it again, point-one-seven—that represents the time it takes, in seconds, to execute a home run swing. Basically, that's seventeen hundredths of a second!

If you want to compare all this with the numbers in other sports, let me say this: Those are only part of the numbers involved. There are numbers upon numbers you could use to calculate the dynamics.

For example, there are numbers related to the strength and height of the batter as well as the strength and height of the pitcher. There's also the rotational speed that a pitcher can put on a ball for some of the more complex pitches. That can go from eighteen hundred to twenty-four hundred RPMs (revolutions per minute).

Humidity and degrees impact the pitch. Wind speed impacts the pitch. Wind direction impacts the pitch. There is also the contact angle at which a bat hits the ball based on a batter's swing. In baseball, it feels almost endless. And yet, in a real way, all these numbers make the sport so pure and just stunning to watch.

Here is another side note—my side note actually.

In researching this, I not only got exhausted, but I also noticed and got a sense that some scientists got exhausted. (For the record, I don't mean Cynthia.) You seem to get some high-precision numbers on the one hand, and then it's kind of a fudge factor on the rest of it: Oh, yeah, well the weight and height of a pitcher also have an impact—the wind speed, the humidity, all these things have an impact.

But here is the one that I just love. I love this number! And I think a lot of people who are baseball fans will also love this number, and that number is 2.9.

2.9 set against 3 to 3.2—Let's take a look.

2.9 seconds—the time it took Rickey Henderson to go from first to second when he was stealing the base. That number, 2.9, is set against the numeric range of 3 to 3.2 seconds.

3 to 3.2 seconds—the time it takes to throw a pitch, have the catcher catch it, and have the catcher throw it down to second base.

So the truth is, as the science or the numbers suggest, you could not throw Rickey Henderson out as he stole bases. And history simply states emphatically that his opponents didn't!

If you want to look at the precision in the sport, here is another number: 6,776.

6,776—the number of home runs in 2019. It was by far the most in league history up to that time.

Major League Baseball even commissioned a study to see if the balls were intentionally juiced up.

Let me write out what they found: "The laboratory experiments using newly developed techniques showed a correlation between the drag and the seam height of a baseball—with the average seam height in 2019 smaller than 2018 by less than .001 inches." That's less than one-one-thousandth of a difference in the seam height on a baseball. That is amazing. They concluded that the seam height was probably the cause of the home run increase. That's how precise baseball can be!

(That report was authored by physics professor Alan Nathan, statistics professor Jim Albert, mechanical engineering and mathematics professor Peko Hosoi and mechanical engineering professor Lloyd Smith.)

So, next, we are going to continue to look at numbers: Numbers and scoring.

I've been writing about numbers and how that concept impacts the sport of baseball like no other. And I suggest to you, it is not even close. This is my second attempt to hit a home run on the numbers aspect that concept modeling (and others today) suggests is underlying all of baseball. So I want you to imagine the following.

What if the commissioner of baseball came out tomorrow and said this: "We're going to make a change in baseball to make it more exciting. And thus, reaching a base is now going to count as one point. You know, we are tired of people getting on first and not getting credit for it. Isn't that our culture today? So we want to elevate the sport. We want to make it for today's generation. So if a player gets to first, that player gets a point. If the player gets to second, he gets another point. Third? Another point. And for a home run, he gets four points. How exciting is that? (...big pause...)

It's not!

Not to mention the outrage, not in just one town but across the USA. Exciting? Definitely not. And that outrage wouldn't just be coming from Cooperstown. It would be coming from across the country, from every baseball fanatic, even from regular fans. And even the casual observer would not be happy.

But don't worry. It's never going to happen in baseball. If you're a fan of other sports, watch out! I know some of you may be already shouting, "Other sports? No way! What are you talking about?"

Well, guess what? Basketball already changed its point system—

in 1979 with the three-point play. I don't know if you remember, but there was a lot of outrage at the time. But it calmed down soon enough.

And what about football? When you turn to that, it was 1958 that the two-point conversion was introduced into college football. But it only became official in pro football in 1994. That is not as dramatic, but guess what? Numbers can and do change in a sport.

A few paragraphs ago, I was writing about the ninety feet from home plate to first base, but what if you were to change the length of a football field? Would there be an outcry if you made the football field a hundred and forty yards? It's an interesting question because a football field didn't start out as a hundred-yard field. It started out as a hundred-and-ten-yard field from goal line to goal line, but with the introduction of the forward pass in 1905, they had to lengthen the field by creating end zones—which were introduced in 1912.

But because some of the stadiums at that college level were already built and set, they had a problem doing that—expanding it. So they created a compromise. They added the twelve feet for each of the end zones but then reduced the field from 110 to 100 yards. So you had this confusing mix right there, but it would eventually settle on being a hundred yards for the main field—goal to goal—and ten yards for each of the end zones.

For the record, baseball executives could change a couple of things, but they'd risk destroying the game. There is one consideration that I am going to write about in a bit that might cause them to change one thing.

But here is what is interesting. You don't actually destroy football by putting in end zones. You actually enhance it. And you don't destroy the game of basketball by adding the three-point play. In fact, for basketball, that change has revolutionized the game—made it more exciting and kept, in terms of fans, the sport growing.

So let's go back to pitching.

The ability to throw curveballs, sinkers, and sliders is a matter of using the rules of physics, the size of the ball, the pitcher's mound, the distance, the motion, and all the energy you generate as the pitcher winds up and makes a throw. And that is all defined and driven by numbers.

It's really hard to throw a baseball at ninety miles an hour. For myself, I think it's even hard to throw a baseball at fifty miles an hour. Eighty? Well, that's starting to separate the men from the boys. And the ones who can make it professionally today have to get it close to ninety-five (some suggest 92.3) and accurately at least most of the time, right?

On the home plate side, that's where it starts to get difficult for the batter. It takes a lot of skill to hit a ball going ninety-plus miles an hour. At a hundred-plus mph, the speed of the pitch changes the nature of the duel.

The fastest pitch on record is a Nolan Ryan pitch at around 108 eight miles an hour. Now, some of you fans might be looking it up and saying: "What about Chapman's?" Chapman did one at 105 mph in 2016. Some consider that the fastest pitch of all time. But did you read the footnote? Here is that footnote: "The fastest ever reliably recorded by the Pitchf/x system." I think there's a little bit of an agenda there, don't you? "Wow! Every stadium ballpark must have one of those Pitchf/x systems from now on." (Nolan's pitch was recorded using a different radar system.)

Look, you can call it what it is—both Chapman and Nolan are great. Period.

You know in all this stuff, whenever you do the research, you always have to look for the hidden agenda. And I'll do a lot of that when I go on to the origin history of the sport.

In this book, we are more focused on pitching in terms of how that element is foundational to baseball. So at ninety miles an hour plus, it's very difficult to hit a baseball accurately. But at a hundred miles an hour plus, even the best professionals—the best of the best—find that hitting is no longer a skill. It is luck. That has to do with the mechanics of the human mind and body. How fast the body can work physically.

Pitching at a hundred miles an hour plus is a big-money skill. And if it keeps on going to 105, 108, or even 110 mph, they would probably, and only under that condition, have to move the pitching mound.

The curve, the slider, the sinker, the knuckleball, the changeup, and all the rest (from our concept modeling point of view) stem from such a simple word. That's the lesson here. It stems from the word *throw*, and it turns into the art form we call *pitching*. That is why the obvious is so important, and it's amazing.

Like No Other Sport—Not An Afterthought

Baseball is sometimes called the perfect sport. Let me just add, "and it's all brought to you by Wheaties," or—wait. Wait! I forgot something.

You see we got lost in all this numbers stuff, and I forgot the biggest proof about numbers. Numbers is also about stats.

The whole point is, from day one, baseball was about stats—driven by the numbers concept underneath it all. But, as I asked earlier, don't other sports have stats? Not like baseball.

Football versus baseball stats—let's take a look:

When football started, you didn't even have stats—just the scores and a sense of what happened in the game. Real stats weren't significant in football until 1932. That is sixty-three years after the first official game.

Here's the funny thing about baseball, and this is true. The first stats appeared one year before the very first professional baseball game. That's how far ahead baseball was: It was even ahead of itself! I don't know exactly how that happened, but there have been so many additions to baseball stats throughout the years that it would take a whole new book to go through them.

But from a concept modeling point of view and *The Obvious Isn't*, here are some of the key things.

Every sport now has stats, but baseball has had its own brand of stats. Baseball has had what they call box scores. Henry Chadwick—highly influential and sometimes called the father of baseball—created box scores. The first box scores appeared in 1859, in an issue of the *New York Clipper*. Just to note it, there were stats before that, but Chadwick took it to a whole new level.

The second point about stats is its relationship to baseball fans. Those box scores, landing in newspapers, have mattered. They have given people something to talk about, and, yes, it is that simple. Baseball's nature has been different. It has had innings. That made tracking stats much easier. In terms of fans, it has allowed them to talk about those averages, those numbers, as they progressed. Some of the stats were kept to the end of the year, but over time they began to be more and more incorporated into the box scores. Those then have shown up in newspapers.

Here is the big shift with stats in baseball. And I have a shout-out to give to Alan Schwarz[5] ; I read an article that points this out from his baseball book called *The Numbers Game*. The biggest change comes down to one player, and everyone knows who I'm talking about. Before 1919 he had been a pitcher and doing well. But his batting was pretty impressive, so they changed him from a pitcher because in that position you don't get to hit or practice as much as you do when you're an outfielder. The change enabled him to focus on hitting. That year he started to bat incredibly well. And his name was Babe Ruth.

His stats were so important that for the first time, stats were suddenly more important than the outcome of the game. Everyone was watching the stats on Babe Ruth: how many home runs he hit.

Here are those numbers: In 1919, he hit twenty-nine; in 1920, he jumped up to fifty-four; in 1921, he hit fifty-nine. And for his career, he ended up with 714 home runs.

It wasn't until Hank Aaron, in an exciting year, that anyone caught up to him and finally surpassed him. How important were stats to the sport of baseball? In the late '40s, we are talking 1840s, a few teams started to hire statisticians. They tracked game stats. And of course, you could then use those stats, and player stats, to impact the game—probably they were used in selecting some of the players. If you ever saw the movie *Moneyball*—a great movie starring Brad Pitt—it demonstrates a later rendition of using stats to impact a game or the quality of a team.

For most sports, statistics have been an afterthought. The proof for me is now in soccer, which is allowing all these new stats—like how many passes a team makes in a half—into their game coverage. I love soccer, but I also have to say this because it also sheds light on baseball.

In soccer, there's no fan who's going to say, "I believe our team will pass the ball twelve more times before the end of this half." It is an afterthought. It doesn't really enhance the game while you are watching it. It can tell you something about a team after but not during the match.

But here is the point: From the get-go, baseball stats were being developed—new ones, bad ones, thrown in, thrown out. That was happening during the second half of the 1800s as baseball developed. And my gut tells me that newspapers really lived off those stats in the sports section. As a regular feature, it helped fans keep up with their favorite players and glue them to a team. It was something to talk about—something to dream about.

Lastly, there is a different kind of number that I will be writing about in the twenty-fifth, or final, chapter of this book. Amazingly, it is a number that is somehow linked to another transcendent concept—the human spirit. It is found in this: One team. One player. One play. One moment—as a player steps up to the plate or onto the field and delivers not just a hit, a play, or even a home run. This is something that transcends all of that—and delivers something above every other number.

That mysterious thing is something that we can all share by our nature as humans, as fans—and we simply love it. I am looking forward to explaining that in detail in that last chapter.

So, I hope I have hit in a few singles in my attempt to make up for those three strikes, but hopefully you're getting an even deeper sense of what numbers mean to baseball versus other sports.

Before we move on, there is a proof I want to mention: When you do concept modeling, you do the concept model, you dig deep, you do the research, and then you set it all aside. And then what you do is you go after external proof—something that shows you some insight, some proof that you have done the model correctly. It's something that in itself is obvious. You start with the obvious, and you end with it.

I set down the model and started to look for that proof. And I found it. And it comes to this old saying about baseball that's still around today: They're always saying *baseball is a game of inches!*

And there you have it. It's the numbers underneath baseball that make it what it truly is today: one of the best sports ever created. Perhaps the perfect sport.

In the next chapter, I'm going to step into the history of baseball, which I think is out in left field. You know what? If I could, I might be tempted to be in some historians' faces like former Baltimore Orioles manager Earl Weaver was, at times, in umpires' faces.

Maybe we'll get a taste of that in the next inning—I mean chapter.

PART II

Introduction to Part II

In part I, we began to walk through a concept model on baseball, meaning we explored some of the concepts that dwell at the heart of the sport. There is still much more to explore there.

But in part II, we will now use what we learned in part I to dive into the origin history of baseball. We will actually use that concept modeling to ask different questions, take a different approach, and then use insights gained in part II to serve as a guide in finding the truth and expand both our concept model and our insights into the sport we all love: baseball.

CHAPTER SEVEN

WHY CONCEPT MATTERS
AND WHY BASEBALL ORIGIN RESEARCH IS
AT RISK

So let me start part II of this book with a request.

I am giving you a little homework to do. But don't worry; it will take less than thirty seconds. I just need you to see some of these names: rounders (especially rounders), cricket, stoolball, English base-ball, (note the hyphen between the words), poison ball, tut-ball and others. Just a quick look will do. I will cover most of it in part II of this book. But as a warm-up, let me show you something about the history of baseball.

First, I do indeed love the research, the historians, and even the resources referenced throughout this book. But as you read this, baseball origin history is at risk. One reason is that there have been any number of definitive findings, such as those with regard to the Abner Doubleday story, that illustrate that what was thought to be definitive regarding baseball's origins turned out to be not definitive. (Like the notion Abner invented baseball in Cooperstown, New York in 1839) It has happened and is still happening with the game "rounders"—this book is designed to put a nail in rounders' coffin forever—and the damage it has done is worse by far than the Doubleday debacle.

While doing a last minute review of this chapter, I did yet another quick test (Retrieved June 2022) and I freely admit, I got Earl Weaver-like riled up. I googled this question: *How was baseball invented?* And here is what popped up:

The game evolved from older bat-and-ball games already being played in England by the mid-18th century.[6]

As you will see, that statement is as misleading as the debunked statement that Abner invented baseball...in a single day! Why? It assumes that no bat and ball games existed *until* Europe itself existed. The truth is, that statement is based solely on limited available documentation—words on a page. But, if we used that logic, we could state that the sun did not exist until some document said so. But what we are talking about are basic, universal things like a bat and a ball. Things as basic as sticks. Things that are round. Things as basic as the sun.

Still, their conclusions are perhaps understandable. Historians were looking for *baseball* as it relates to bats and balls—physical things. I was looking for the *essence* of baseball in both its physical and, more importantly, its abstract nature. (It was *batball* not the word *baseball* that actually helped me step closer to its essence.)

But how many refutations will baseball fans allow before true skepticism seeps in? That skepticism is already here, and outsiders can feel it in some of the words used by researchers today. It's found in the couching of words—the "it's possible but" and "it was once believed." And it's even evident in double talk, as examples below show.

We know that revisions happen in every field, right? Newton's gravity theory was overturned by Einstein's view. Baseball origin history has changed and is bound to change. And given the nature of baseball documentation itself, it is much harder to lock down what is craved by many fans, particularly many American baseball fans: something clearly definitive on the origin of baseball. It may not be on the surface—what true fans talk about—but it is buried deep and is a potential source of pride. Science has definitive experimentation, equations, and testing that lock down its theories. Paleontology has fossils. Perhaps we need something new, a kind of fossil, if you will.

But first, let's do this:

A Review of What is Out There as of March 2022

Many, if not most, encyclopedias—such as *Encyclopedia Britannica, New World Encyclopedia,* and *Wikipedia*—have all, at one time or another, suggested with certainty that baseball comes from Europe. Rounders has been the candidate with the longest reign at the top of the list as the source game. It has only been by the influence of Block's *Baseball Before We Knew It: A Search for the Roots of the Game*[7] that some online sources have begun to pull away from the notion that rounders is the source of baseball. However, the theory that rounders was the source of baseball is a dominating influence, even today. (Thus the reason I did that last minute test in June. Hold the presses!) Let's review some examples:

1. Britannica, "Rounders" (Retrieved: August 8, 2021)

It reads:

> Played in England since Tudor times, it [rounders] is referenced in 1744 in the children's book *A Little Pretty Pocket-book* where it was called Base-ball.[8]

First, it is odd right off the bat, (another accidental pun but immediately claimed as intentional) because the same *Encyclopedia Britannica* states that the Tudor dynasty ended in 1603. That's over 140 years before this Tudor proclamation. (For the record, there are—but less than a handful—of mentions in actual Tudor times of youths playing ball, stoole ball, and tutte, but no base-ball.) Regardless, this encyclopedia entry is troublesome and here is why:

It is a bit like saying **water polo** is referenced in a 1744 children's book . . .where it was called **surfing**. Folks, it is either rounders or base-ball. Don't say base-ball and then suddenly say, "Oh, they really mean rounders." I don't buy that. Not for a second. And you shouldn't either.

More proof? Jane Austin used the word "base ball," not rounders, in her book, *Northanger Abbey*[9] , which she wrote around 1789 and got published in 1818. Still, some sources stated that in using the word *base ball*, Jane really meant rounders. Like this example, there is definitely a lot of rewriting of history or retrofitting selected European games following any time a new European candidate is the chosen source. Specifically, I mean rounders and by extension, it's apparent derivative in the United States, which was called townball, as we will see.

Also, there is another hidden issue buried in the *Britannica* entry that dovetails into the next citation example:

2. New World Encyclopedia, "Baseball" (Retrieved: 2/16/2022):

> **It is generally agreed that modern baseball is an American development from earlier British games, such as rounders, with possible influences from Cricket.**[10]

So I, for one, don't agree. But, as I say to everyone, "Who cares what I think?" Still, questions remain: What makes something credible? Something certain versus possible? How can documents alone do that when documentation around and on baseball's origin history is extremely limited? In point of fact, the documentation is so limited that this question arises: Is it the research or the interpretation of the research that matters most? And isn't this double talk? It states it is an "American development" and then adds "from earlier British games," so how does that make it American? Then, there is this line from *New World*'s entry just before the one above:

> **The distinct evolution of baseball from among various bat-and-ball games is difficult to pin down.**[11]

In this line, *New World* expresses doubt on pinning it down, but then it goes on to pin it down—in its very next sentence—with rounders and cricket. And that is a massive problem: It states the research is unsure, and then it states that the research is sure, as in, "generally agreed upon." That fuels skepticism.

Viewed from a slightly different angle, is *New World* saying it is "difficult to pin down" yet that it's appropriate to pin the source down to Britain? If so, why pick Britain when almost every other country had a stick (or hand as a stick) and a ball game: Germany, Scandinavia, Sweden, Spain, and many others, including France. If it is "difficult to pin down," why not stay away from pinning it down until it is absolutely certain? And then there is the biggest problem: American baseball is not from Britain.

From a concept modeling point of view, many of these problems stem from a lack of digging into, analyzing, and capturing the concepts buried deep in baseball—not the superficial aspects of baseball, but baseball's essence.

3. "Cricket," Encyclopedia Britannica (Retrieved 2/17/2022)

> The earliest reference to an 11-a-side match, played in Sussex for a stake of 50 guineas, dates from 1697. In 1709 Kent met Surrey in the first recorded inter-county match at Dartford, and it is probable that about this time a code of laws (rules) existed for the conduct of the game, although the earliest known version of such rules is dated 1744.[12]

Cricket is not baseball. So why did I put this piece in here? It is for anyone thinking, "Well, these European games like rounders needed time to develop." Or it's for anyone thinking, "It was too early for sports in Europe." But this cricket entry belies that claim. Cricket was well formed by 1744. That strongly suggests Europe was capable by 1744 of forming a fully-developed baseball-like sport. But it didn't.

4. "The Official History of Baseball," Major League Baseball Productions, Volume 1, 1994 Covering the years 1869-1969, volume one of two was released in 1994 and states the following:

> The roots of baseball can be traced to colonial England where they played a game called rounders.[13]

MLB is great, but I wanted to point out this excerpt because it suggests that the notion of rounders as the source of baseball has been plaguing baseball origin history for decades.

5. "Origins of Baseball," Baseball-reference.com (Retrieved May 26, 2020) Under the Cricket and Rounders sections, it reads the following:

> That baseball is based on English and Gaelic games such as cat, cricket and rounders is difficult to dispute.[14]

Amazingly, of the three, the best case for it could be made for cat, as we will see. But cat is not baseball. Cricket is not baseball. And we'll get to rounders shortly—it is simply a disaster.

6. "Rounders" Wikipedia, (retrieved: 2/16/2022) Here it is:

> Consensus once held that today's baseball is a North American development from the older game rounders, popular among children in Great Britain and Ireland.
>
> American baseball historian David Block suggests that the game originated in England; recently uncovered historical evidence supports this position. Block argues that rounders and early baseball were actually regional variants of each other, and that the game's most direct antecedent are the English games of stoolball and tut-ball.[15]

Note that rounders is still there as a "regional variant." But just two years ago, as I did research for my book on baseball, I found this in the same *Wikipedia* entry (retrieved: 9/17/20):

> References to baseball date back to 1700s where in England it was known as a game called rounders. Rounders is referenced in 1744 in the Children's book *A Little Pretty Pocket-Book* where it was called baseball.[16]

The difference between the two entries highlights the impact of David Block's excellent work and book. Even though the research is actually great, truly exceptional, there are problems here.

Tut-ball and stoolball are definitely not the antecedents or origin of baseball. Stoolball is clearly the predecessor of cricket, which is an entirely different sport. And tut-ball? No. The concept of a base is totally different than that of a tut. Tuts were brickbats, basically chunks of stone or pieces of brick; one was not likely to step on them at a faster speed owing to injuries that would have been more serious at that time. And given their size, it would be odd not to have used several pieces together in a pile. In fact, one 1811 trap-ball illustration shows what you could call brickbats as pieces of stone and rocks forming a pyramid-like pile. (As we will see, that is actually significant.)

Above all, it is more than likely that tuts were more like field markers, especially in some of the early games in which players were required to run the *entire* circuit without stopping—perhaps touching the tuts as they cornered by them and perhaps not. But they were not bases; as we will see, the concept is just not there.

So what is the origin of American baseball? The existence of this relatively new entry in *Wikipedia* suggests that for the foreseeable future, there will always be new evidence, new theories, and new documents that may knock another pretender out of the running as the source of baseball. It just feels like it has happened too often.

Again, the first origin story had Abner Doubleday as the inventor of baseball, but uncovered evidence proved otherwise. (That was a victory for true research, but a sad one.) Then David Block put a big dent in rounders. But if and when rounders collapses, townball (an acclaimed derivative of rounders) should collapse.

So there is a big problem, which is clear to see from the outside when you step back and put all the source/origin candidates of our baseball together; it sounds something like this:

They threw something toward someone who used something to hit it back somewhere and run, so that must be the source of American baseball?. . . I don't think so.

It is not the physical things, or general activities that make our baseball what it is; it is the shift within the deeper concepts underlying and defining those physical things and activities.

As an analogy, the iPhone is not a phone—the name "iPhone" is simply there for marketing purposes. Even though it is super popular, the phone functionality within the iPhone is just another app. Why is that critical? Think of the former top of the cell phone industry: Nokia. Every company like Nokia that did not make the transition from a cell phone to a computer-with-apps collapsed in the marketplace. This is a critical business point: **Cell phones are not iPhones and iPhones are not cell phones.**

Similarly, none of these European contenders made the right kind of concept-based shift in their games; so they just aren't baseball. Baseball is driven not by the physical, but by the abstract concepts: just like the cell phone concept versus the computer-with-phone-app concept.

A way to think about concept-based analysis is this (as mentioned): It's about letting baseball itself tell us its own story and reveal its deeper and wonderful secrets.

It just seems to an outside fan that once one European contender collapses, another, even less likely candidate—I might say "pretender"—is then chosen simply because it preceded our baseball in time.

7. *Baseball*, a Film by Ken Burns

In Ken Burns' monumental documentary film called *Baseball*, the narrator states the following at twenty-one minutes and five seconds in (21:05):

> **Baseball's most direct ancestors were two British games: rounders, a children's sport brought to New England by the earliest colonists, and cricket, a stately pastime divided into innings and supervised by umpires.**[17]

First, Ken Burns is brilliant. That documentary film is brilliant. Truly epic. But that statement is just not true, and it colors everything that follows on baseball's origin within that documentary.

It serves as an analogy for the rest of baseball origin's history itself—the ship started off in the wrong direction. Amazingly, if you do make the course correction—with rounders and to a lesser extent, with cricket as well—you can actually use Ken's fantastic documentary as yet another proof that baseball comes from the United States, not Europe.

The documentary focuses on townball (a derivative of rounders) with this statement at 22 minutes and 33 seconds in:

By the 1800s, townball and its many variations were played nearly everywhere.[18]

Unfortunately, that is just not true. And it highlights the bigger problem: Documentation on baseball's origin is not just limited but extremely limited, yet we make these big leaps. I do as well, so I have to catch myself often. The point is not to win a debate but get it right.

Despite the fact that there are relatively few documents on these games, research finds a few documents that mention townball but only a couple on something like "round-ball." Then suddenly it seems a decision is made that round-ball is just another name for townball, just like "base ball" in that 1744, *A Little Pretty Pocket-Book*, poem apparently (but not really) becomes code for rounders. That kind of switch has shown up many times.

Suddenly townball absorbs other games like round-ball, or just ball—any and all names of games subsequently found. It becomes retroactive. Every other game is now just a "version" of townball—and how does one dispute that off such a great documentary?

As mentioned, townball wins what is a *documentation battle* in a world where documentation is extremely limited. Townball, as a community event, naturally also wins the hearts of newspapers and reporters who would have covered town festivals but would have not covered stories on kids playing base ball or literally stickball in the streets at that time. The end result is that it makes it feel like townball was everywhere when it wasn't everywhere.

How do I know? There were actually two townball games.

One was the community-festival, pony-ride-like game the whole town played together, which hints at the origin of the word "town" in the name townball. It is the reason the documentary states the following:

Eight to 15 men played on a side; sometimes as many as 50.[19]

Both the problem and the proof is found in that one statement: There is a duality there—eight versus 50. No credible sport, or even a league per se, would have 50 people as players on the field, but a hometown festival or town carnival would. By the way, that was never the case for baseball, and the documentary even tells us about that: It mentions that larger crowds were coming out to watch these New York base ball players playing at the Elysian Fields in Hoboken, New Jersey. But that crowd was on the sidelines, not on the field of play. Having a crowd playing the game itself was indeed the case for townball—clearly a community, hay-ride-like amusement at first.

Then there was a second townball, which was a version of itself: It was more than likely spawned from this idea: "Hey, that town-holiday-festival game was fun. Let's form a group to play that ball game more regularly. I want to show off some more!" From the second version of townball, some direct games like the Massachusetts Game (called Town Ball in its rule book) would eventually emerge; apparently it was sourced from round ball in New England. In one last research quest I found the illustration below created by Charles Stanley Reinhart[20] around 1870. I have inserted a section of it that points to there being two townball games. (Last minute find on 06/19/22)

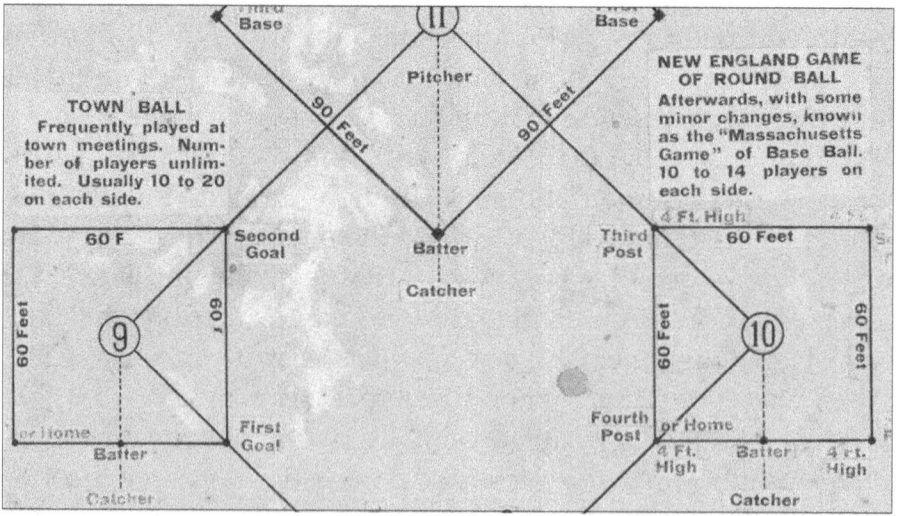

Fig. 9: "The American origin of baseball" Illustration by Charles Reinhart, 1870

Note that the Town Ball caption to the left reads: Frequently played at town meetings. Number of players unlimited.

But there were other entirely separate, different games from townball (or round ball), and one of them coming from New York City would be townball's downfall.

Another quick example or proof is found within the same film at

20 minutes and 59 seconds in:

Children have hit balls with bats as long as there have been children.[21]

If Baseball's statement on children above is true (mostly it is), you have to ask this: Why start the origin story in Europe? Why not before, even centuries before, back in Roman or Egyptian times? The answer simply points to documentation as the deciding factor. Shouldn't the nature of baseball itself have some say? And there is a way to do that using the game's own "DNA"—basically, that means deconstructing what truly makes baseball, baseball.

The DNA of Real Baseball

I introduced part I by reminding anyone reading this that there is a separation between the physical and the abstract. And a look at the essence or abstract nature of our American baseball allows me to state the following emphatically.

None of the games coming from Europe carry the concepts that are at the core of our American baseball.

It is like DNA. The DNA of baseball is either in these games from Europe, or it is not. It is either in rounders, or it is not. It is not. It is either in stoolball, or it is not. It is not. It is either in cricket, or it is not. Close, but it is not. As an analogy, Homo sapiens' DNA is either in Neanderthal man or it is not. It is not. (Even in that analogy, I am also not talking about being close, but about a game-changing, extinction-level difference.) Concept modeling is about digging down into the DNA of baseball.

Now that we have set the playing field and ballpark, let's deconstruct and analyze the evidence.

Concept modeling something like baseball is about discovering, then locking down, the essence of something. And I know that gets a little foggy, but real essence is found in the abstract world—not just the physical.

Concept modeling, the practice of it, dictates that you set your own ego down—and I have to do that all the time—and ask the obvious questions without assuming you know the answer. Why? Because the obvious actually isn't!

The great thing is this: When you set all that down and deconstruct something from an essence point of view—which is found in the nature and structure of concept—guess what happens? You arrive at something that is almost always different, much deeper, and more logical—even more beautiful, and, definitively always obvious. What is interesting about this book (also in *Concerning the Nature and Structure of Concept*) and what I just wrote is this: We just did a lot of that—in part I of this book.

But here is the most amazing eureka moment—which happens all the time when you delve into abstract essence—our very two first and crazy-obvious questions from this very book, led us to bat and ball, and batball.

That gave me the next question, as well as the first question, that everyone should ask to find the truth about baseball's origin history: the concept model, our "fossil" on baseball, strongly suggests, even dictates, that you need to ask this question first:

Why isn't it called batball?

That means when I started my review on the origin of baseball, I was not looking for *baseball*. Rather, I was looking for *batball*.

And as it turns out, that simple twist—that simple question—radically changed how I would look at the history of baseball and how I would uncover many of the mistakes in that history. It led me to the truth about the origin of American baseball.

Here is one hint: American baseball does not come from Europe.

That becomes obvious once you have a concept model on baseball in front of you.

Next, we are going to use concept, or the discipline of concept modeling, to go deeper into the history on the origin of baseball.

And I promise you this: the secret to unlocking the missteps in the history of baseball may also come from a massively unlikely source, the comedy duo of Abbott and Costello.

Now how cool is that? Find out! Keep reading!

In the meantime, to wrap up this chapter, just remember the "o" in obvious. We just went full circle. That is because we started with the obvious, and we end with the obvious.

The Obvious Isn't.

SEVENTH INNING STRETCH

WHO'S ON THIRD? NO, HE'S ON FIRST?

I mentioned that at the concept level, baseball is actually batball—and that it matters. So that became the objective of my origin history search. Find batball.

To me if you are looking for the word *batball* and find *base-ball* instead, you are shocked. If, as I assume many researchers did, you are looking for the word *baseball* and you find "base-ball," you are happy, if not thrilled, at the discovery. The problem is that looking for the word *baseball* will throw anyone and everyone off the right trail.

Who can we use to best explain the issue? Two famous comedians perhaps? To explain this, about words, I need to turn to two great guys Abbott and Costello. Remember them? Does what I have to say surprise you?

Even if you haven't seen them, Costello is the short funny one. Abbott is the tall straight man. Together, they were popular here in the US in the '40s and early '50s. According to *Wikipedia*, they were the highest-paid entertainers in the world during World War II or, as the once-famous orchestra leader Lawrence Welk said once, World War "I—I." So maybe it's been years since you saw their routine, but you will recognize this one.

As it turns out, Abbott and Costello probably hold the key to the essence of the problem with baseball history more than anyone on the planet ever did. Give them a listen using your imagination:

> **Abbott:** You know nowadays they give these baseball players a lot of funny names.
> **Costello:** Yeah, a lot of goofy names.
> **Abbott:** Like Dizzy Dean,
> **Costello:** Boopy Barber
> **Abbott:** Well, let's see, on the team we have, uh, Who's on first, What's on second, I Don't Know is on third...
> **Costello:** Are you the manager?
> **Abbott:** Yes.
> **Costello:** You know the guys' names?
> **Abbott:** I sure do.
> **Costello:** Then tell me the guys' names.
> **Abbott:** I say, Who's on first, What's on second, I Don't Know's on third and then you...
> **Costello:** You the manager?

Abbott: Yes.
Costello: You know the guys' names?
Abbott: I'm telling you their names!
Costello: Well who's on first?
Abbott: Yeah.
Costello: Go ahead and tell me.
Abbott: Who.
Costello: The guy on first.
Abbott: Who.
Costello: The guy playin' first base.
Abbott: Who.
Costello: The guy on first.
Abbott: Who is on first!
Costello: What are you askin' me for?

In that baseball skit, they created one of the greatest comedy routines of all time. Bar none. But in that Abbott and Costello skit, the "who" is used as a name, not a pronoun. In other words, the word *who* doesn't mean what Costello thinks it means.

That is the problem with the research. Guess what? The word *base* in the 1700s and before doesn't mean *base*.

Base meant something else.

CHAPTER EIGHT

BASE, AS NOT IN "BASE BALL" BUT BASEBALL

Let's Visit the Use of the Word "Base"

The appearance of the word "base ball" in a poem in a 1744 Children's book, *A Little Pretty Pocket-book*, by John Newberry has been used to help reinforce that baseball's origin is found in Europe. And why not? There it is—the actual word "base ball"—for the first time in history (barring new discoveries).

Now we can use that "Who's on First?" routine from Abbott and Costello to address the point. Again, in their routine, the use of the word "who" doesn't mean what Costello thinks it means; Abbott was not using it as a pronoun.

Likewise, the word "base" as found in that 1744 poem is trouble—a source of real confusion. It is like the *who* in "who's on first?" The word *base* in the 1700s and before doesn't mean *base* as we know it today.

So What Does *Base* Mean in 1744?

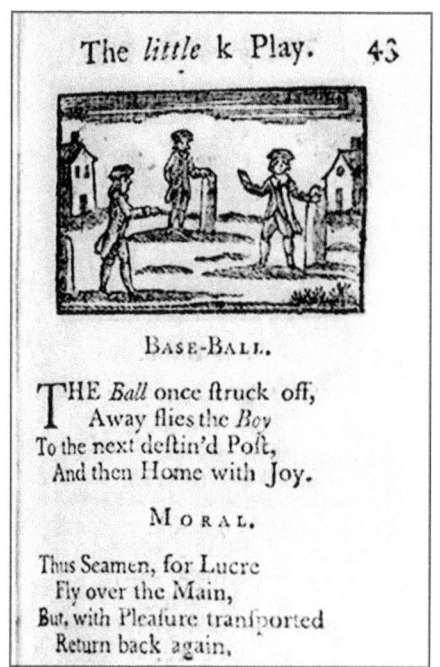

Base comes from the Latin word basis, which, yes, at first glance and naturally, contains the word *base* in it. But it really means—and especially back then meant—pedestal.

And the proof of that statement is overwhelming.

As we will see, the concept of a real baseball "base" never appears in any of these early European games.

Fig. 10 *A Little Pretty Pocket-book, by* John Newberry, 1744 First American edition. Worcester, Massachusetts: Isaiah Thomas, 1787 Courtesy, Library of Congress

In fact, this proof is actually right in the book that some are using to make their case. Their case? Meaning to support that our baseball is of European origin.

Fig. 11: A Little Pretty Pocket-book, 1744 (1st American Ed, 1787, See p 66) Rare Book & Special Collections Division of the Library of Congress, Washington, DC

Let's focus on an enlarged version of the illustration as seen above the base-ball poem.

Pedestals are Not Our Baseball Bases

That illustration shows kids or young adults playing a game with a ball. One looks about to throw the ball to someone else standing in front of one of three bases on the field. But look at those again!

Those are not bases there, folks. Look at them! They are three pedestals. They look like they're three feet high, little Washington Monuments. Not bases.

Pedestals are oriented towards the hand not the foot, as noted by the center player who has one hand on the pedestal. For the record, the player to the right has no bat. He is using his hand as a bat. Lastly, the pitcher or feeder as some may have called him is about to pitch, or better stated, throw the ball underhand. That's not baseball. At that time the word "base" meant "pedestal."

Of course, those shapes are recognizable if not obvious. And I certainly understand that some researchers may say or even claim that those pedestals were indeed obvious at their first glance. But the point is very clear: Many if not most have used this poem to suggest, even make the official case, that baseball originated in Europe when it did not. As mentioned, a baseball exhibition presently at the Library of Congress suggest this image "...debunks the great myth that baseball was born in the United States." But where's the bat? Baseball must have a bat or it is not baseball as shown in chapter three. Also, look again. A pedestal is not a base. Who, What, and I Don't Know aren't on first there.

Additionally, from a concept modeling point of view, a pedestal is not an early-baseball-history base. Rather, it is a completely different animal from the base used in our baseball. By extension, the divertissement shown in the illustration is not baseball. Not even close. Are those the very first baseball caps too? The point be made. The problem is this illustration has been used to, if nothing else, leave a *feeling* that baseball originated in England, whereas pedestals go back to Rome, Greece, Egypt and, yes, prehistory.

Now if you want to excuse it by saying, "well, it was early in the game," keep in mind that pedestals are still used today in a sport that looks similar but is very different from baseball. That sport is cricket, which was already a fully developed and rather competitive by 1744. (That's the reason I touched upon it in part I.) So, significant development of the game could have happened with "base-ball" but it didn't. "Early in the game" is not an excuse.

Amazingly, cricket's pedestals are still called stumps today—a remnant from stoolball—three poles stuck in the ground connected by two bails at the top. The bail is one of the two smaller cylindrical sticks placed on top of the three poles to form a wicket. The pitcher, called the "bowler," is trying to knock one of the two bails down. That is actually a different concept than the pitching found in American baseball and a key differentiator as an entirely separate sport.

A quick note on stoolball: Apparently, at first, stoolball (stoole ball) used tree stumps, with the *pitcher* trying to *strike the stump*, not strike the batter out. From a concept-based view, stoolball is a direct link in the evolutionary development of cricket. Like many, if not most, of these European games, stoolball developed a round layout—yet another historical hint that Europe was thinking in terms of round playing fields—which we will see is critical to proving where baseball originated.

Back to the illustration: It points to a way of thinking about bases. Again, note that one of the players has his hand on top of the pedestal. Our bases are foot-oriented. Soccer and volleyball both use about the same sized ball. One uses hands, the other feet—but they are not the same sport.

The elegant dress of the participants suggests the game shown was just a game, not sports-oriented, meaning that no player was going to dive head-first into those pedestals at top speed—something critical to the concept of professional competition found in American baseball today.

Pedestals were hand-oriented. Taller. You see that in rounders and townball—they used sticks in the ground. What are sticks in the ground? Like those in cricket, they are the remnants of pedestals. Those as shown in the 1744 illustration would have been cumbersome to transport to open fields for a game. So these latter games used sticks, keeping the notion of a hand-oriented safe spot (or just markers).

Perhaps the illustration also speaks to these games being played in cemeteries, which is referenced in some documents. Perhaps it speaks to community parks, or town squares, memorial sites, or areas displaying statues, memorial pedestals, tombstones, or monuments. No stonemason back then was making a living constructing three-foot-high Washington Monument-like pedestals for boys or adult "base-ball" games. Historically speaking, if they did, a few of those pedestals would have survived and served as evidence.

If we are looking for the origin of baseball in 1744, shouldn't we also look for the origin of pedestals themselves? Pedestals make sense historically. In ancient times, some pedestals were rocks set up to form a small pyramid-like structure. They marked a location of significance; most likely, some stood as memorials. Later, they served as the "base" for statues or as standalone objects.

In prehistory, you could also easily imagine that if one rock was placed on top of another on top of another, boys might have tried to knock down those rocks by throwing other rocks. Did cavemen and cavewomen have "teenagers" who liked to play occasionally? Of course they did. It was more than likely that throwing a stone accurately was an important skill used in self-defense against predatory animals or even human predators. In that way, pedestals go back almost as far as sticks.

Going forward in time, you come to trapball, where an illustration from 1811 in *Remarks on Children's Play* shows perhaps brickbats or piles of stones used as bases. That is basically one chunk of stone (brickbat), or little chunks of bricks, assemble into little pyramids (pedestals). I suspect tut-ball used brickbats, but as markers, not bases. At that time, many of these early games required you to run around the entire circuit layout without stopping. What does that mean? They served as "markers," not bases—just touching a base as you run by is not necessarily the same as declaring it a safe spot.

The historical question remains grounded in a concept-*based* (there's that multifunctional word again) question. What is a *base*?

Perhaps the most important bit of evidence is the illustration on how townball, the so-called derivative of rounders brought to America, was played in the United States. There are at least two pieces of critical evidence with regard to where real bases were created. The one below comes from the *Base Ball Player's Pocket Companion*, 1859.

Townball's Stick? That's Not Our Bases

BASE TENDER.

Fig. 12: *Base Ball Player's Pocket Companion*,[22] (Boston: Mayhew & Baker, 1859), page 31 Courtesy Baseball Almanac (see next page)

This was the Massachusetts Game, understood as a version of the game townball as indicated by another document, *The Rules of the Massachusetts Game (Town Ball)* (see next page) from 1858.

Now, note the stick in the ground in the illustration above. From a concept modeling point of view, it is yet another proof that baseball comes from the United States. Real *bases*—the concept of foot-or-slide-friendly, stat-plat (what I call stat-platform), athletically oriented bases—were not in the Massachusetts Game (Town Ball). Again, historians have often pointed out that townball was rounders transplanted here in the United States.

Townball's Non-Diamond Layout

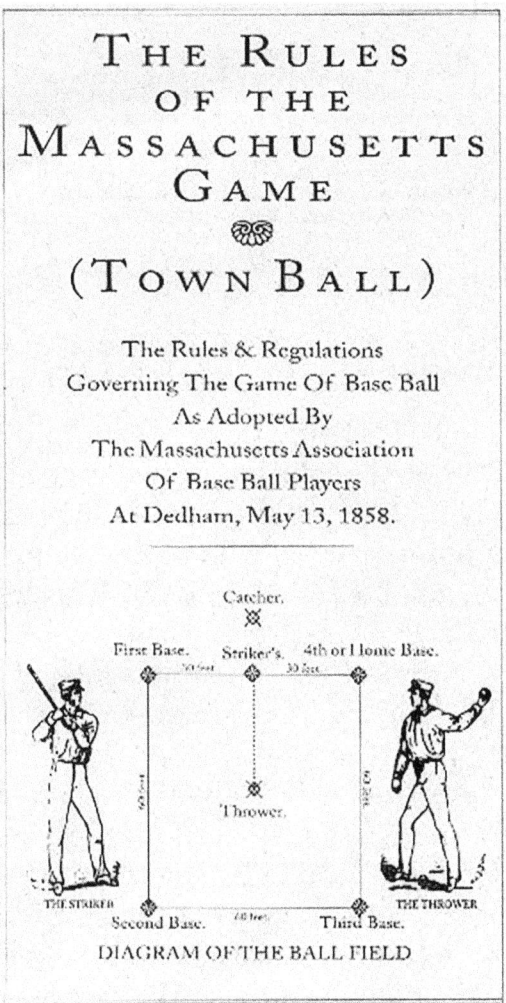

Fig. 13: *The Rules for the Massachusetts Gam (Town Ball)*,[23] May 13, 1858
Courtesy of Baseball Almanac, www.baseball-almanac.com

On the previous page is that rule book, *The Rules for the Massachusetts Game (Town Ball)* from 1858. We see the same drawing style for the players on either side of a diagram as was found in *the Base Ball Player's Pocket Companion,* 1859.

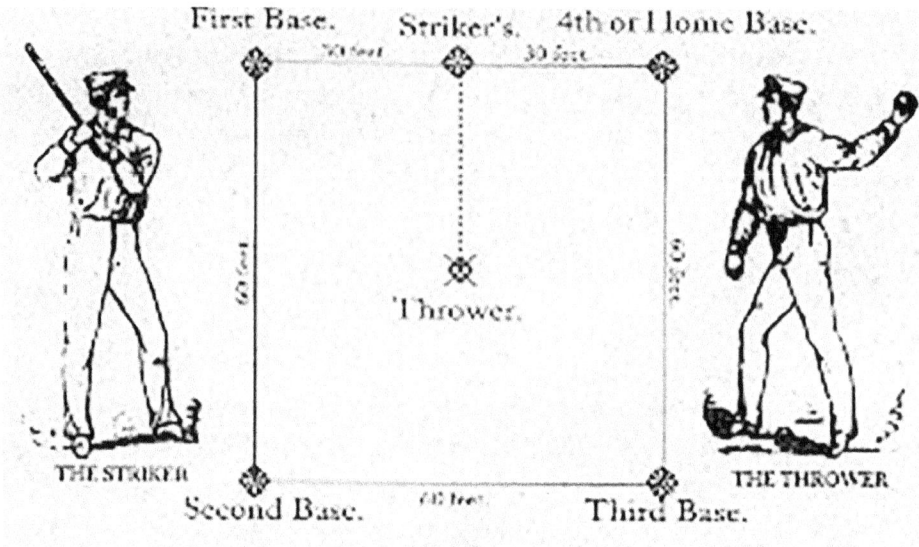

Fig. 14: Close up: *The Rules for the Massachusetts Game (Town Ball),*[24] May 13, 1858
Courtesy of Baseball Almanac, www.baseball-almanac.com

But you may notice that "the thrower" (not pitcher) also has no glove. Additionally, note that the bat shown in the illustration to the left is not a baseball bat as we know it. So the question is, from a concept modeling point of view, when does a stick become a baseball bat? Giving them a benefit of a doubt, it is close, but not close enough. The emergence of real baseball bats were still about 26 years away from the year 1858. These illustrations reinforce the premise that neither townball nor rounders are the source of American baseball.

The Massachusetts Game (Town Ball), died off, as all versions of townball died off. That is telling. It is an evolutionary-like survival of the fittest, and townball didn't have the stuff to beat this emerging thing already here but soon to be called baseball. Did townball, or rounders, have the DNA of our baseball? No. It was just not there.

But we are not done; we can also derive something else from the rule book illustration: it shows a box-and-one-shaped layout. So you have to ask—and we will shortly—if townball is derived from rounders, why isn't this diamond-shaped? In other words, where does the diamond shape for rounders from the description of rounders in the 1828 book, *The Boy's Own Book,* come from? That is interesting—worth noting. We will get to that in detail in chapter ten.

Anyway, this illustration points to a physical reality: No bats. No bases. Also, no baseballs. None of the real physical attributes that make them the real equipment used in American baseball are present in townball or rounders. In rounders and townball, you would throw the ball directly at a player to get the player out.

If a player, while running the Bases, be hit with the Ball thrown by one of the opposite side, before he has touched the home bound, while off a Base, he shall be considered out.[25]

One other note: The overhand throw, as you see in the illustration, was not our American baseball pitch. Here again we find a concept-based issue: It was still different than our baseball pitch. For the record, in 1828, rounders rules state it was an "underhand gentle toss," and townball early on as a community game started out with an underhand toss. More specifically, the Massachusetts Game as played in the United States at that time, when some local clubs were forming, was simply an overhand throw—still not an attempt to strike the batter out. (As mentioned, there was also a similar game called round ball played in New England then as well.)

Now by the 1850s, interests in games were growing, perhaps making them even more newsworthy unto themselves. There is an article in 1856 in the *Porter Spirit of the Time* that suggests that games in Massachusetts and New England that were using the overhand throw were at that point doing that with "vigor"—the article notes that the games in New York were pitching the ball with vigor as well (though underhand).

But this article about northern US games is more like covering an earthquake; it was why the article was written in the first place—it was showing a shift in the game.

Again, that could have happened with rounders in England, but it didn't. It shows townball was attempting to adapt to US tastes and interests. It would fail. Again, where is that all happening? In the United States.

The Ultimate Base-Layout Comparison: The Massachusetts Game (Town Ball) Versus the New York Game

The Massachusetts Game (Town Ball) used a box-and-one layout—and townball stemmed from rounders. But the same *Base Ball Player's Pocket Companion* from 1859 also shows the layout for an entirely separate game: the New York Game—and, wow, it was diamond-shaped. (See Fig. 15, next page)

In other words, there was a different game out there and in direct competition, if you will, with townball.

The layout also proves that the New York Game did not come from townball. Otherwise, the layouts would have been the same, and they were not.

In the Ken Burns series Baseball, writer Roger Angell states the following at about 23 minutes and 21 seconds in:

The truth of the matter is that baseball was an urban game almost from the beginning. Organized ball was played by men in cities near saloons.[26]

Combined with the layout from the *Pocket Companion* on the next page, that quote from Roger Angell suggests that our American baseball was a game that emerged from cities and city streets; it was an "urban game."

If true (and we will see shortly that it is) then rounders and thus townball were not the source of our American baseball—there was a separate game around: "The New York Game" which shows a diamond shape.

The New York Game has a Diamond Shape

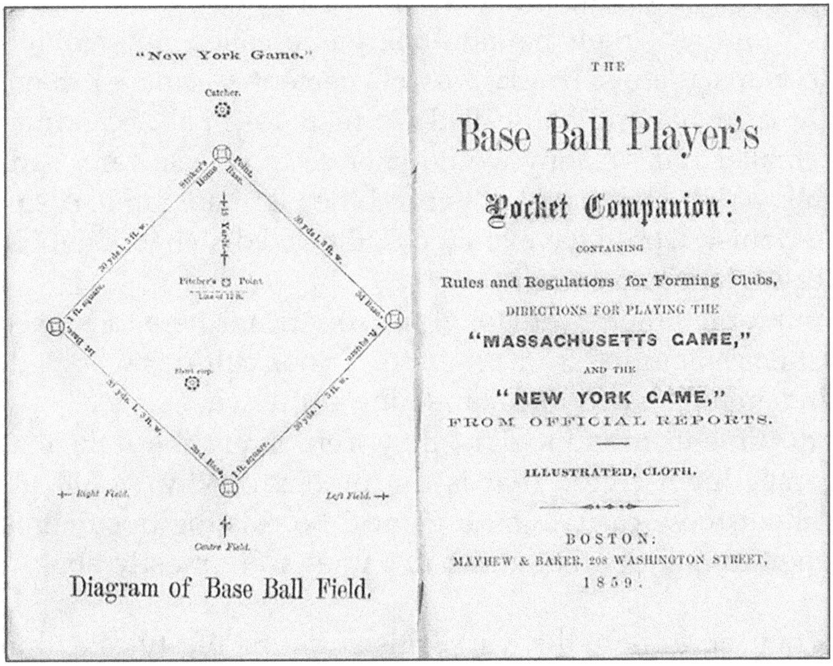

Fig. 15: *Base Ball Player's Pocket Companion,* (Boston: Mayhew & Baker, 1859) Courtesy of Heritage Auctions, HA.com

The title page (right side) above also proves one decisive thing: That the Massachusetts Game (Town Ball) was a version of "base ball," and not the other way around, as some have suggested.

Again, let's refer to what the Ken Burns' *Baseball* narrator said at 22 minutes and 33 seconds in:

By the 1800s, townball and its many variations were played nearly everywhere.[27]

This title page from 1859 (above, right) proves the exact opposite. It was all falling under "base ball" not "townball." "Base ball" was the generic term that had many, many variations and only one of those was townball.

And that makes much more sense from an immigration point of view as shown through population data. The US colonies were not solely replants from England. For example, it was the Dutch who created the colony of New York. French and Germans came to the United States as well. There were Irish and Scottish immigrants too.

If England brought rounders to the United States, the French probably brought their bat-and-ball game called poison ball, and the Germans (Pennsylvania was 60 percent Germans) may have brought their bat-and-ball called German base-ball. Scandinavians (their smaller 1700s colony would later become Delaware) had their longball, which may have influenced the German game. Also related, the Danish would have longbold, the Swedish had långboll, and the Norwegians had slåball.

Don't forget, there were longtime Americans here too—meaning generations stemming from all these various cultures who had been here and amalgamated into something entirely new.

In documents found to date, they were rarely about the bat-and-ball games themselves. That is the problem: Why would anyone write about these casual youth games? So existing documents that happened to mention bat-and-ball games were mostly about other things:

   a. They were about the war: British officers' lifestyles within colonial-war prison camps.
   b. City ordinances prohibiting these window-damaging games—frankly, they were more about the windows than the bat-and-ball games.
   c. Or they were writing about community festivals, and low and behold, that meant townball, which was a community-festival game first. Not a sport. Townball was not everywhere, but new towns and community events and gatherings were.

Reading the Massachusetts Game (Town Ball) rules from 1858, we can note that it was shifting its game play with the overhand throw. But why was townball in America making that shift? And why didn't rounders make that shift before in England? The answer represents an evolutionary twist: It was not that townball was influencing our US games. It was that our US-based games were influencing townball. But it was too little, too late. Relatively speaking, townball died off shortly after the game rules publication. And why not? The diamond shape is cooler. Way cooler.

The page from the 1859 *Base Ball Player's Pocket Companion* makes it clear that the book was about choosing between the Massachusetts Game and the New York Game when creating your local club. For these two contending games, it was an evolutionary-like competition—it was game on! Do you go with the Massachusetts Game (Town Ball) as listed or this New York Game for your club choice? Is there any historical reference calling the New York Game rounders? No.

Perhaps the final evolutionary switch in its name would be the word *base ball* itself. *Base ball* (space between base and ball) was to be condensed into *baseball* as the lasting name of a specific US sport.

We will come back to pitching within the Massachusetts Game shortly, but I need to write about the most important, yet overlooked, pieces of evidence on the origin of bases.

Evidence on the Root of Real Bases: The Most Important Interview in Baseball's Origin History

So, what is a stick in the ground? It is the remnant of a pedestal—and again, it is not foot-oriented; it is hand-oriented. The illustration from *The Rules of the Massachusetts Game* shows that townball did not have bases. That means real bases were developed here in the United States. And the amazing thing is that there is proof.

Historically speaking, the word *base* does not define our US baseball base until William Wheaton— he is one of the key figures of baseball in the USA-—gives an interview in the late 1800s. When he reflects back on the Knickerbocker Rules and their creation—those are the rules for American baseball he helped create—and how they played baseball, early baseball in the cities, in all different places, he makes it clear.

That interview is the first instance where a significant contributor to the creation of US baseball mentions they had bases, which he explains are "sand bags" (bags filled with sand.) There you go. Now that statement is so unimportant that it makes it the truth. And what I mean by that is no one is thinking, "Oh, base. We have to be looking at that. That's really important. I'd better watch what I say about it."

He was just telling the truth. Well, they wanted to create or establish bases which were bags filled with sand. But that is the first time you are hearing about a real base. Bottom line!

And that only happens in America.

In those days, of course, you had to create your own bases—there were no Dick's Sporting Goods stores. But now, for the first time and like the "accurate diamond," we see that they were making choices that defined this game as something very different, driven by a specific, elevated competitive objective at the game's core.

Below is part of Wheaton's interview; it is from the *San Francisco Examiner*, November 27, 1887. For the record, his name was not directly mentioned, but based on evidence within the articles, researchers have concluded that this is Wheaton. Here is the critical segment of that critical interview:

> **The first step we took in making baseball was to abolish the rule of throwing the ball at the runner and ordered that it should be thrown to the baseman instead, who had to touch the runner with it before he reached the base. During the regime of three-cornered cat there were no regular bases, but only such permanent objects as a bedded boulder or an old stump, and often the diamond looked strangely like an irregular polygon.**
>
> **We laid out the ground at Madison square [sic] in the form of an accurate diamond, with home-plate and sand bags for bases. You must remember that what is now called Madison square [sic], opposite the Fifth Avenue Hotel, in the thirties was out in the country, far from the city limits.**[28]

That interview exemplifies why my look into the origin of baseball took eight months. Not planning to do research at the time, I read that interview casually and I had not connected the dots. Also, I did not track it the first time I read it—there you go! Proof that every baseball researcher reading this is better at research than yours truly!

When I went back to read it again, unknowingly from a different source, that critical paragraph was not there. It had been edited out. In other words, it was so "not important" that it was cut out in order to shorten the interview section in that article. It was not intentionally deceptive; it was obvious that the paragraph was just not seen as important.

Later, and for a second time, I decided to go back and find the full-length version of the interview and—wham!—suddenly it was all there. This time I saw the implications clearly—and it was the concept of batball that helped open my eyes since it was forcing me to look at the concept of base in every game I read about—and I did not find the real one, a real base, anywhere until I saw it in Wheaton's interview. There it was: a sandbag. There are specific concepts that make an American base different and real.

When Wheaton says that "during the regimen of three-cornered cat there were no regular bases"—in other words, cat wasn't it and didn't work—note that he doesn't say three-based cat. To him, cat was a "regimen," not a sport. The word cornered also implies something more like markers or, as he states, "only such permanent objects as a bedded boulder or an old stump." Those were not baseball bases either. That was not what Wheaton and others were looking for—boulders and stumps did not fulfill their competitive needs. There was to be a major shift, in the direction of a new competitive sport and soon to be a club. The organizational nature of a club speaks directly to the improvement and development, if not creation or even revolution, of game play and locked-down rules.

Wheaton goes on to, well, complain about cats by saying that "often the diamond looked strangely like an irregular polygon." That shows the diamond shape was something they thought about and already knew. They were looking for something specific and different—something they had seen and knew about but now wanted to do with precision: a diamond shape. He says, that they "laid out the ground at Madison square [sic] in the form of an accurate diamond, with home-plate and sand bags for bases."

Wow. As I read it again today, in February 2022, it is all there. It is layered into his interview and his statements: He was discarding the three-cornered cat, and neither a stump nor a boulder was what they wanted.

A stump? Remember that, historically, stumps were first mentioned in connection with stoolball, then later in cricket—meaning that all the games coming from Europe were all thinking along the lines of stumps, markers, sticks in the ground, and pedestals. He then referenced Madison Square, with the "square" unintentionally reinforcing the notion that the city's geometry was probably influencing the layout for bat and ball games in US cities like New York. Even though Madison was a park at that time, it was still square in dimensions—at least that is how he remembers it.

So they made sure it was an "accurate" diamond, which implies that many in the city were already using the diamond shape—he saw it played like that in the city and liked it. Madison Square could be a place they could get the layout perfect. He doesn't mention it casually. The diamond-shape mattered to him. Notice he doesn't mention townball at all. Box versus diamond? They wanted a diamond layout.

The interview proves one thing and also strongly suggests another. First, it proves bases come from the United States, not Europe.

Second, it suggests that this was the real game of baseball. There is clearly an intentional creation seen here. Through men like Wheaton, a new game was being intentionally formed, but also reconstructed from urban, basically street, games (and perhaps others), already present and thriving in the big city. They were taking the best ideas (game-play elements) and creating something new that would soon be housed in new base ball clubs in the late 1830s and 1840s. This was something more athletic—more for adult play—the kind of competitive play that he mentions made the regimen of cat too dangerous for adults.

By combining various pieces together, this new evolutionary game play was not found in other games that were falling under this generic term of "base ball," as it was used at that time; this was the continued development of a distinctly US game in a city in which a distinctive American competitive spirit was alive, thriving, and growing. A base ball club would be an organized way to bring this better game play to life, by locking down new rules of a game influenced by what America was about: more competitive, more precise, more athletic.

They were on the hunt for something you could play at a different level. More accurately, they were creating it themselves. Real. American. Baseball.

Survival of the Fitness

Appropriately, the article reveals that there was a competition between various existing games. Earlier in the interview, Wheaton mentions cricket and all other games competing for the hearts and minds of young adults and that none of them were enough exercise for them:

> **We had to have a good outdoor game, and as the games then in vogue didn't suit us...[29]**

He mentions "games," meaning plural, or a lot of games. This new breed of game, for athletic, competitive-minded, full-strength adults as he describes it, was soon to take a small, short-lived organizational step as the Gotham Base Ball Club, where Wheaton helped craft some of the new, different, and early rules. Smart guys like Wheaton were building a new game by taking the best of what they had seen in the streets while excluding what didn't work in these other games.

This-game-versus-that-game popularity competitions were also happening in Massachusetts, perhaps Philly as well. We know that because townball dies off. And the existence of this stated townball club in Massachusetts didn't help.

Wheaton was a significant player and leader in the Gotham Base Ball Club in 1837—so he touches upon the "thirties" within the article—and the all-important Knickerbocker Base Ball Club in 1845.

Wheaton was where the real game—with its specific DNA—of American baseball was present and forming in New York and influencing places like Boston too. As we will step into soon, a publishing partnership between Boston and New York book publishers for *The Boy's Own Book,* 1828 (which they brought over from England the next year) shows that Boston and New York were connected by interest in these games. The *Baseball Player's Pocket Companion* title-adjacent illustration (Fig. 15) supports that.

In reading Wheaton's interview, the world of baseball seems to come to life: He is telling us how something new, different, athletic, competitive, and aimed at adults had formed here in America.

CHAPTER NINE

ABBOTT AND COSTELLO SHOW US A BEAR OF A PROBLEM

Agendas make the history nutty. You can almost hear that nuttiness in some of the claims made about where American baseball comes from:

In Germany: You must believe it started in zee fatherland, ya?
In England: We will play it on the beaches. We will play it on the landing grounds. We will play it on the fields and in the streets. We will play it in the hills. We will *never* surrender our claim to baseball!
Or maybe it's **Cooperstown, New York, USA**: You mean just down the street? You mean here where baseball was invented in just one day by Abner Doubleday? Golly, Mr. Local Cooperstown Drug Store Manager wearing a funny paper-boat-shaped white hat. You mean I can have an all-American hot dog and a root beer float right here? At this counter inside your pristine drugstore? Then I can walk to the National Baseball Hall of Fame and Museum from here? Is this heaven, Mr. Drug Store Manager?

Agendas make the history nutty. And in concept modeling, you must always look for those agendas. And even your own agenda (mine included) can be a problem. Knowing that will help you find the true essence of a thing—and keep you from missteps.

But to shorten all this to under seven hundred pages, I'm going to turn it back to the two guys who are truly the PhDs of comedy: Abbott and Costello.

So maybe it's been years since you saw their movies, but you will recognize this often-repeated scenario.

I'll just do my version.

Abbott and Costello find themselves in their grand wilderness hotel suite at a luxury mountain resort about to embark on their great wilderness vacation the very next morning.

It is nighttime, and they're talking in their room, planning the last details: A little bit about this being bear country and how Costello doesn't want to come across any bears. "No bears," he says. "This will be great," Abbott assures him, "Fresh air. Nature. Tomorrow we become frontiersmen." "But no bears," Costello insists.

But suddenly the lights go out. Abbott wants to find out the problem from the front desk, but he doesn't exactly tell Costello he is leaving the room. Abbott leaves the room from one door while—of course!—a bear steps into the room from another door. He is man-size or bigger, walking upright on two feet, but because it's dark, Costello can't see anything. So he starts fumbling around the room looking for Abbott, using his outstretched hands.

In other words, he can only feel his way around the room, and sure enough, when he reaches out again, he taps the back of the bear, and he thinks he's found Abbott. Then he says things like, "Oh, there you are. For a second I was worried. Wow, you put on your outdoor coat already? We don't head out till tomorrow. But come over here. I think I have some matches with our camping equipment."

Of course, the bear follows too closely for comfort, but Costello doesn't get it yet and says, "Wow, you really need some mouthwash. Your breath is horrible!" Finally, he lights a match, turns, and sees the bear for the first time, and you guessed the rest.

"Abbott!!!" And he runs off full throttle with the bear chasing him right out the door!

That represents a typical scenario for Abbott and Costello. But right there is a hint of a significant problem with the history of baseball.

First, it is an expected Costello-like mistake. Researchers are looking for "baseball," so anything they touch in a nonfiction book, in a novel, in a newspaper, in anything written, or in anything drawn in illustrations must be baseball. So when they do that, they find something. They decide it *looks* like baseball, (it uses the word too) so it must be our *baseball*. But what they find is the bear instead.

In Hollywood scriptwriting, there is a saying—and I am paraphrasing—you must be willing to kill all the words, to kill the scene you love, even if you have worked on it a long time. We all make mistakes, so you have to be willing to let go of all the work you did, all the training you have, all the all you have, in exchange for letting baseball, not the superficial, reveal its deeper truth.

Baseball Research & Gravity

Up front, I've got to stress one thing that is really important. The historian work on baseball is actually very cool. It's well done. It's a demonstration of solid, hard-fought research, great thinking, and serious work. The methodology used by researchers in most cases is great, and I love it.

On the other hand, and you probably knew I was going to write this, there is one thing we have to recognize. Conclusions are different than research. Second, and historians also know what I am about to write: some of the history is agenda-driven.

One subtle but obvious proof—you can see it by just reading the statements. Some historians are looking for the source of baseball *in* Europe. Some, as we all know, have been looking for the source of baseball *in* America.

No. No. No! All of that smacks of agenda. However small, however unintentional. It will lead us to the wrong conclusions.

A spaceship headed from Earth to Mars will be hundreds of thousands of miles off target if it is even one degree off at the starting point. That is why there are course corrections in space travel.

That one degree in baseball history—you won't believe it—is the word "in." That's right. The word *in*. You can't look for baseball *in* this country or *in* that country. You can't look for baseball *in* this game or that game. You simply have to look for baseball. Not baseball *in* this or that.

But you can't avoid that mistake unless you have a fossil in front of you. In our case, unless you have a concept model of baseball in front of you before you start your look back into its history.

Right now, I want to give another shout-out to David Block, who wrote an exceptional book called *Baseball Before We Knew It*. Go buy that sucker! It's kind of fun reading. I really wouldn't have been able to write at least part of this book, without his work. Period. His comprehensive research—years in the making—is exceptional.

It doesn't mean, however, that I agree with everything David says. But the great thing about David is that, in his book, he says the two things that are so important.

First, he says, and I am paraphrasing, that a lot of the research is based on the limited materials that are out there. That's an important, if not critical, point.

Perhaps a lot of you have a sense of the history of baseball already, but there is an asterisk here. Here is what I mean: If you're researching World War II, you have millions, if not billions, of documents, interviews, and other source materials to go through. In baseball, there are probably fewer than six hundred documents (and I am giving myself breathing room with that number) that relate to the history of baseball. I could be wrong, but most of those aren't even significant. They are just mentions of the word.

The second thing about David is that you get a certain sense about this from reading his book: There's a humility about him. I am paraphrasing, but in his book, he suggests that some of the research may have to be updated. That's what we're trying to do with this book.

Of course, with all the attempts—the books, the articles—you know we're bound to make mistakes. And the history they found on baseball is just fascinating. It just happens to be wrong.

So what is it that we are doing differently? We are looking at its essence—the abstract nature of the sport.

The essence of baseball is not found in words, novels, quotes, or any other aspect of writing. But let me say something about it from our concept modeling perspective, letting baseball tell us its own story:

Baseball, the essence of baseball, couldn't care less about someone's opinion—academic, research-based, or otherwise. It couldn't care less about baseball experts, TV personalities, baseball players—not even encyclopedias, dictionaries, novels, or articles. And it doesn't even care if you are a concept modeling guy like me. Fact.

Baseball is baseball. It's like H_2O or gravity. It just is what it is. Gravity couldn't care less what we think is true or not about it. If we called it by another name—a Chihuahua—it wouldn't change its essence or nature.

Newton may be the greatest scientist of all time; I consider him the greatest. We still used his work to get us to the moon. But his view of gravity as a force was replaced by Einstein's view of it as a warp in space-time. By the way, that too may change, for the record.

Now, nothing in those statements makes any of their work, or them, less great. They are the greatest. But reality is not dictated by research. Essence dictates reality. It stands apart. It is we who have to discover what that essence is. Essence is found in both the physical and the abstract.

That's why we did the concept modeling first. In concept modeling, capturing the essence of something is what gives you these insights. You're going to create and build a product? Concept model the abstract side of it.

Surprisingly, you are not looking for words, for shapes, or even a bat and a ball. You are looking for the essence of the sport, which most of the time and with almost everything in life is not found in the physical—such as bat and ball—but in the abstract things, such as specific athletic skills, found at the heart of the particular sport.

If you don't have a "fossil" in hand while doing research on baseball, you take a big risk: It is like Costello looking for Abbott in the dark. In our case, that fossil is a concept model on baseball—defining the essence of the sport.

In the end, that kind of work also has a proof, and it is in this fact: essence always turns out to be obvious.

CHAPTER TEN

THE DESCRIPTION OF ROUNDERS IN THE BOY'S OWN BOOK, SECOND EDITION, 1828, IS
"FALSE ADVERTISING"

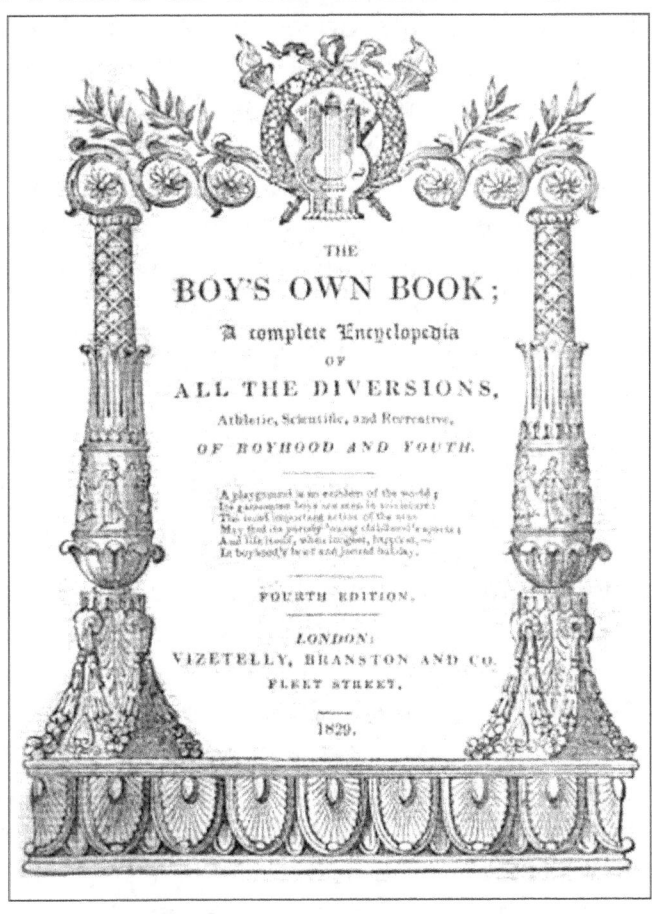

If you know anything about the history of baseball, you know that most of the time—perhaps better stated, for the longest time—they said that rounders is the source of American baseball. Sorry. It is just not true.

Again, as a reminder, here's what most of the research still states online. For the longest time, it was like a religious mantra. This one happened to be, as I pointed out, from the *Encyclopedia Britannica* only last year. In fact, as I took a look again in April 2022, the entry was the same:

> **The descent of baseball from rounders seems indisputably clear-cut.**[30]

Next, I am kind of throwing it all in here so you get a snapshot of the general argument: Well, it's that rounders had a baseball-like bat. No, it did not. And it is categorized as a "bat-and-ball game," so it must mean they are related. No they are not. And since it came first, in other words, before American baseball, our American baseball must be related to rounders. No, it's not.

To explain that, I will use and look at rounders from our new concept modeling point of view. And as I said from the get-go, let's let the essence of baseball serve as our guiding light into all this research.

These are two of the most extraordinary sentences in all of baseball origin history:

> **In the west of England, this [rounders] is one of the most favorite sports with a bat and ball. In the metropolis boys play a very similar game to it called feeder.**[31]

Innocent enough, right? I mean, come on—it reads (and sounds) fine. But it is not fine. And upon deeper inspection, it is not even close to fine.

The excerpt above is from the 1828 second edition of *The Boy's Own Book* by William Clarke. As you may know, this excerpt and the rest of the description of rounders in that book were used to make both a direct and indirect case that baseball originated from rounders and thus more broadly from Europe.

Again, the great research of David Block shows that this entry is copied verbatim, over and over, from as early as the 1830s to even in the 1900s in books like *The Book of Sports* by Robin Carver (Boston, Lilly Wait, Colman and Holdman, 1834); *The Boy's and Girls Book of Sports* (Providence: Geo P. Daniels, 1935); and *The Boy's Book of Sports* (New Haven: S. Babcock, 1935). The three were mentioned in David Block's book.

That one entry's influence is so deep that the common baseball fan using Google for a simple search and review of baseball's origin would probably be convinced that rounders or Europe is the source of baseball; you actually have to dig, and dig deep, and then dig even deeper to find cracks in historical claims. The research problem is that the repetition of the rounders entry from 1828 left nonprofessional researchers with the perception that there are many sources for the evidence, but it all actually stemmed from only once source—that 1828 book.

By indirect, I mean that even if rounders is finally discarded as the origin of baseball, the fact of the English birth of rounders still leaves the misguided impression that baseball must have come from some game from Europe anyway.

There is more to the description of rounders, but the above is sufficient for our first swing. When concept modeling is done on these two innocent-looking sentences, what they reveal is striking, like evidence unwittingly left at a crime scene by a perpetrator.

False Advertising

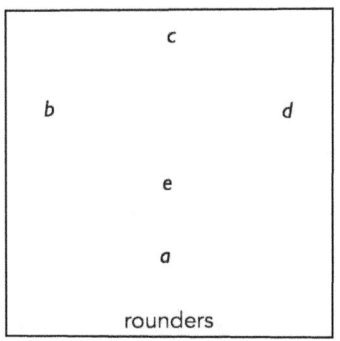

Fig. 16: *The Boy's Own Book,* by William Clarke, Second Ed., 1828

To make matters worse, to the left of this widely heralded and leveraged description is an illustration that shows a diamond-shaped base layout for rounders which, when all of the circumstantial evidence is examined, reconstructed, and concept modeled, is just not possible, as you will see. **It is actually impossible.**

Let's take an umpire- or CSI-like look at the evidence. Here we are going to use concept modeling (a concept-based analysis) and see what it reveals.

Foul Ball: Rounders a Favorite? Hardly

The excerpt states that rounders was "one of the most favorite sports" in the west of England. A bit of hyperbole was in vogue as a writing style at that time, but that just meant not many readers would have noticed the serious issues hidden within those lines.

To put this quote into context, remember that this description of rounders is contained in a book about the *favorite* games or sports played by youths in England around 1828.

When you consider this excerpt using the metaphor of a crime scene, it is a little suspicious that the author places extra, if not great, emphasis on the phrase "most favorite." Why not just say "favorite?" Why state "most favorite" when that is assumed by its inclusion in a book about English *favorites*? Was it just a promotional-like spin driven by contemporary style or a subconsciously driven cover up?

Two Strikes Right off the Bat. Here Is Strike One

The statement that rounders was only played "in the *west* of England" means that the game was not played in four-fifths of a country approximately the size of Alabama. To be clear, that means it was played in an area equivalent to, or as small as, one-fifth the size of Alabama.

Now you may be thinking, "that's OK," as every big endeavor has a small beginning, right? But upon second glance, the excerpt also states that rounders was *not* played in any of the cities located in that smaller region. Say what?

That's right, rounders was not even played in the cities in that— one-fifth the size of Alabama—area. In fact, it is amazing; and if you are detective-minded, you'd probably stop in your tracks as I did, think, then smile—you're on to something. Already, there is definitely something very, very suspicious going on here.

How do those two lines make it a favorite? They don't. Why? Because it also takes their misstep further by mentioning the name of the game that was the favorite in the cities in the west: feeder.

Strike Two: The Second Line Mentions Feeder. Why Do That?

The inclusion of feeder is very suspicious. In fact, it is a big red flag. Baseball is about fun, and concept modeling uses both thought and concept experiments, even worked-up scenarios, as detectives might use to develop insights into what happened. So indulge me with this insert:

How Detective Colombo Would Have Played It

SCENE INSERT:

Let's say I use my imagination, and I ask you to play a part. In this scene, I am at your apartment. I dust off my raincoat even though I live in Southern California, where it hasn't rained all summer. I make my excuses and am ready to leave your apartment when I ask you for a favor:

I ask, "Would you mind indulging me for a second? You see, I am off to watch my son play basketball, which they play in an unusual way at his school. Can you just ask me about it?"

Now here is your part. "Sure," you say. "So, how do they play basketball at your son's school?"

And I quickly reply, "Inside their gym."

I wait a second. Then I add, "But, you know, next to that gym there is a wide-open field. And on that field, my son and the boys and girls there play a ton of flag football. You see, once they gather there, a couple of them go get sticks and mark out the boundaries while others create little tuck-in-your-belt flags out of two-inch-wide tape."

But suddenly, you stop me and say, "But you asked me to ask you about basketball, not flag football!"

I stand there in silence. I wait. Then I add, "My point exactly!"

I turn to walk out, only to stop, and turn back to you one last time and say this: "You see. Why would whoever wrote that rounders description in that 1828 book, second edition, even mention the game they called feeder, when the whole point of that entry was to describe rounders, not feeder. Why?"

END SCENE.

Back to Our Book

My point exactly. Why even mention feeder? If rounders was a most-favorite, would that have made feeder a "most-most favorite?" So why is feeder in there?

Why put that line in there unless the writer or editor felt compelled to—even if for a very good or practical business reason? As a detective, you might suspect it was put in there to assuage the citizens in those cities—potential buyers of the book—in the west of England who already knew the following:

(a) Rounders was not played in their cities and thus was not popular.

(b) It was only played in the countryside.

So how does mentioning feeder make rounders not just a favorite, but make rounders meet an even higher standard by their own wording, a "most favorite?" It doesn't.

Round Versus Round Versus Diamond

The insertion of feeder damages rounders' case in another unexpected way as well: Why did rounders as in "round," have to mention "round" feeder, while displaying a "diamond" shape for its layout?

Feeders Definitely Follows the History of European Games: It's layout? Round

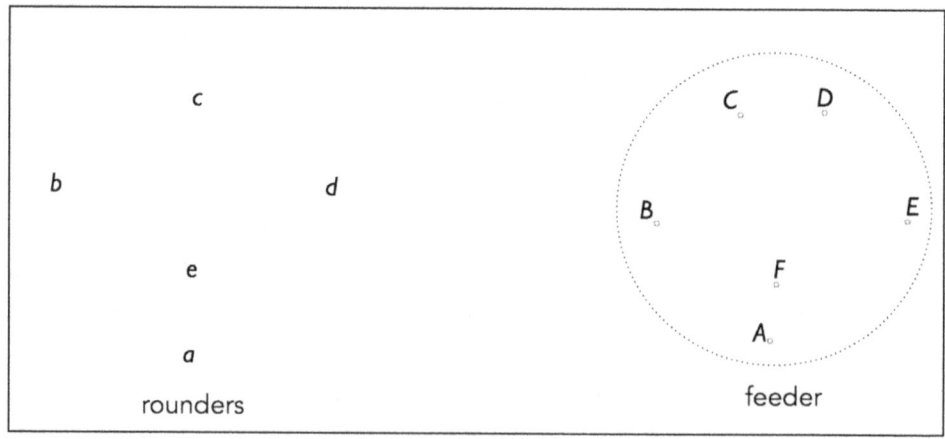

Fig. 17: Rounder layouts is from *The Boy's Own Book*, by William Clarke, 1828; feeder layout from later editions. Dotted round circle added to feeder by Perez for emphasis

Feeder to the right has a visibly round shape (I have added the circle for emphasis), and you will notice that rounders has, visibly, a diamond shape. Yet, by the book's own admission, rounders was "very similar" to feeder. Again, it does not say "similar" but "very similar." What is there to be *very similar* about if not the layout at that time?

So the case against rounders just got a bit worse. And it's about to get a lot worse.

Rounders Doesn't Even Make the First Cut

Guess what? Amazingly, rounders didn't make the first edition of *The Boy's Own Book* in 1828. That is stunning considering that the excerpt starts out by saying it was one of the "most favorite sports." In other words, the fact that rounders didn't make the first cut would be a bit like not including basketball in a first edition of a book on the most favorite sports played professionally in the United States.

So What Happened? The United States Happened

In that same year of 1828, rounders made the second edition of *The Boy's Own Book*, but—and it is a big "but"—that was the edition that was also going to US publishers: One in Boston partnered with a publisher in New York.

Any baseball author who has dealt with book publishers already knows this: Publishers always ask what in your book will relate to the target market? In this case, the US market. Why do they ask that? Because servicing a particular readership is how publishers make money. That will never change. Their success or failure depends on it. Publishers were not so different in 1828.

At the time, US publishers would have naturally asked for inclusion of any game similar to the bat-and-ball games played in the United States at that time. What in your book can relate to our market here in Boston and New York? Do you have a game that looks a little more like this—what we play in the streets here in New York City?

Wanting to be successful, those US publishers would have described bat-and-ball games from New York City and Boston. Games played by boys and perhaps young adults in the square city parks, open lots, fields, and especially streets. **Especially young boys. Especially the streets.** Why? It's **boys**, as in *The Boy's Own Book* afterall.

More importantly, and it is more than probable, those US publishers would have described a diamond-shaped base layout used in those games in Boston and/or New York City, where the big-city geometry probably influenced the layout.

First, did the United States have bat-and-ball games already? Yes. A major finding by the great MLB Historian John Thorn in articles and in his book *Baseball in the Garden of Eden* supports that. Thorn found a city ordinance from 1791 from Pittsfield, Massachusetts; it was written to prohibit bat-and-ball games near an official town meeting house. And that was 37 years before 1828 and that second-edition release of *The Boy's Own Book* by William Clarke.

Pittsfield, Massachusetts, was approximately 153 miles from both Boston and New York, though I would argue that logic suggests that the games spread from those more populated cities to Pittsfield and not the other way around. (We will revisit that ordinance again later.)

A diamond-shape layout was almost certainly created here in the United States. The geometry of bigger cities, as they were designed in the United States and not Europe, suggests as much. The growing size, population, and urban living situation of New York City does indeed look like fertile ground for what historian Roger Angell called an urban-inspired game. Bigger space. Bigger streets. A simple comparative analysis of city layouts in Europe versus those in New York and Boston seems to support that.

There remains yet more and more damning evidence, but for now, when you add the fact that by the book's own description, rounders was not played in the cities, you find that the argument is not even about the United States so much as the book's own description of rounders.

Combining all the analysis, which we will continue to roll out, we will see that there is zero chance "round" rounders had a diamond-shaped layout. Zero chance.

Early 1800s European Countryside Didn't Inspire a Diamond-Shaped Base Layout

Landscape paintings of pre-1828 England suggest that the environment would not have inspired a diamond-shaped layout for the game of baseball.

Don't think of it as you would today, with our biased view leaning toward a diamond shape given the base layout we use for baseball and softball.

How the heck does anyone get a diamond-shape out of this?:

Fig. 18: "Exeter," (England) in Beauties of England and Wales, Artist Unknown

When you imagine stepping out into an open country landscape of the 1700s or 1800s in Europe, with its wide-open, perhaps even hilly, rural settings, the first image that comes to mind is *not* a diamond-shaped game layout. And, according to its description in the 1828 edition of *The Boy's Own Book*, rounders was played in the countryside—not in cities such as Exeter.

A Quick Game Summary So Far

To have a diamond-shaped layout shown next to the description of rounders in the book is not credible for the following reasons:
- No diamond-shaped layout appears in any European game before appearing in the description of rounders in *The Boy's Own Book* from 1828.
- Earlier than rounders, games such as stoolball had a round layout. By 1829, using more stools, they often had a "circular" layout for those stools.
- The second edition of *The Boy's Own Book*, is one of the first, if not the very first, book to mention rounders, yet it suspiciously reads as a rather sophisticated, fully formed game.
- A countryside landscape would not have inspired a diamond-shaped layout. And by the book's own description or

admission, rounders was played where? In the countryside. Not in the cities.
- *The Oxford English Dictionary* (a powerhouse in research) published its first edition in 1884. *The Boy's Own Book* was published 56 years before, leaving it half a century to drive and expand its influence.
- *Rules of the Massachusetts Game (Town Ball)* (Fig. 13) shows a box-shape, yet they say townball came from rounders, which shows a diamond shape. (That's a non-sequitur, folks.)

The bottom line? There is no document that mentions "rounders" before 1828. There are only latter-day research and encyclopedia suggestions that some older word like *base-ball* really meant rounders. That bait and switch was not good for the integrity of research.

An Umpire Call

The staggering influence of rounders in that 1828 *The Boy's Own Book*, led many to assume rounders had these traits:
    (a) It had been around for perhaps hundreds of years.
    (b) It was the foundation for other games that were just variations of rounders.
    (c) A name/word substitution was acceptable because of this.

Baseball—our baseball—is not so much found in the physical, but in the abstract. And here are some umpire-like questions that will help with us getting clarity on the difference between our baseball and these other, pre-1828 games:
    1. Where are the stats in rounders?
    2. Where is the world series of tut-ball?
    3. Where is the baseball pitch concept in stoolball?

Ah yes. We all know that baseball is about stats. Here is the most amazing thing about baseball and stats. We often talk about games in their infancy, but unlike any other game—football didn't have stats till 63 years after its first official game—our baseball was born with stats. As mentioned in chapter six the first stats appeared one year before the very first official baseball game. Baseball was not just born with stats, baseball was conceived with it.

Other sports certainly have stats, but they were actually an afterthought. The amazing thing about baseball is that it is the stats that created the sport of baseball. Whether conscious of it or not, real baseball founders were thinking about the sports' precision—specifics that allowed stats to take hold. The distance to a first base, the nature of a diamond-shaped layout, the position of the pitcher, the hardness of the ball and bat. Those physical things were driven by an even deeper concept, inherent in that game from its creation—something the game of rounder did not have.

I will get to that deeper, specific concept in Chapter Twenty-five, but for now, the concept of stats was, is, and always will be a core concept at the heart of this sport we call baseball.

Where were the stats in rounders? They were just not there!

Not the Crime of the Century in the 1800s

By making just two moves to alter feeder's round layout, London publishers or the author of *The Boy's Own Book* in that 1828 second edition could easily give rounders a diamond-shaped layout feel. Here is what I mean:

1. Move the c from rounders to in between the C and D of feeder.

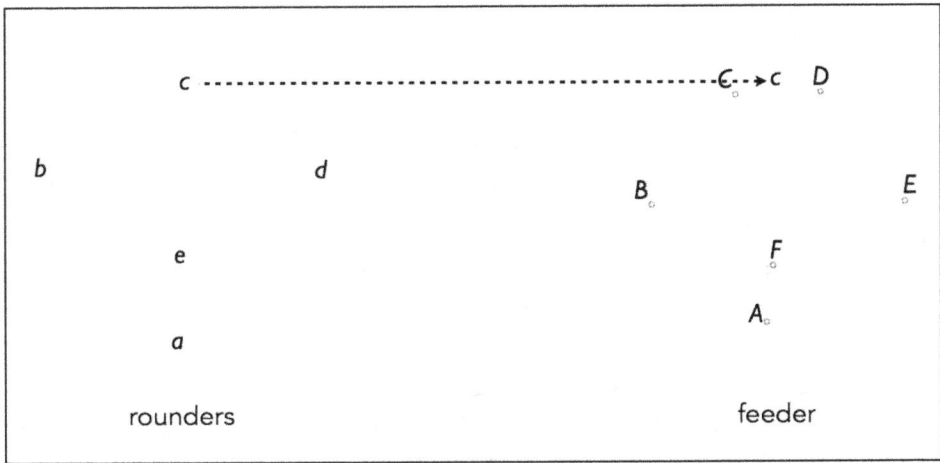

Fig. 19: Rounders shape taken from *The Boy's Own Book*, 1828; feeder shape to the right taken from later editions, with modifications (dotted line, and small c) made by author Perez

2. Second step: delete the big C and D from feeder leaving just the c.

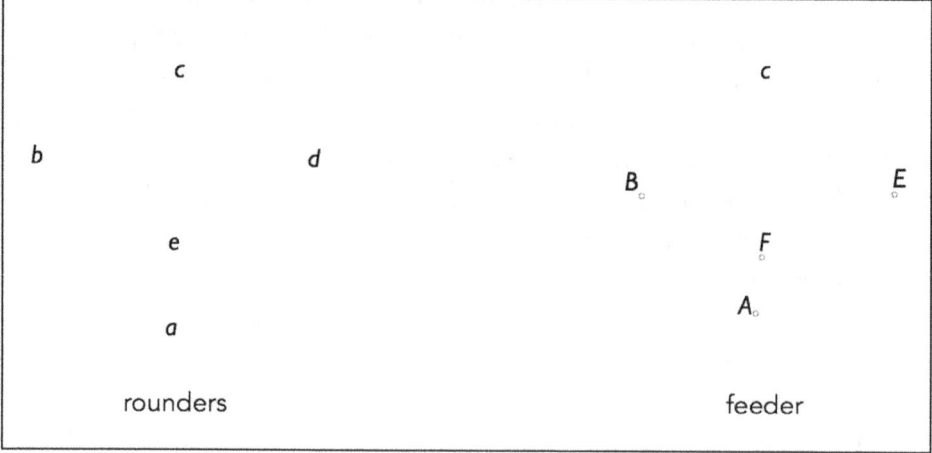

Fig. 20: Rounders layout taken from *The Boy's Own Book*, 1828; feeder layout taken from later editions

3. And you are there: an easy step to false advertising. A diamond.

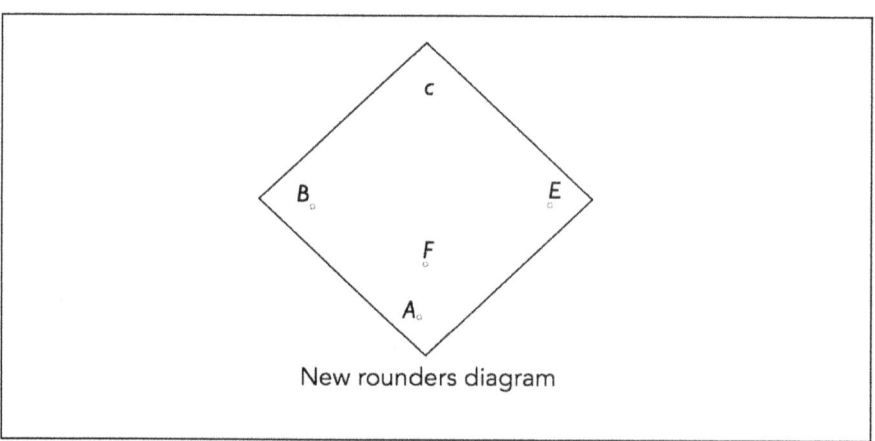

Fig. 21: The diamond shape above has been added for emphasis by author Perez. Also, Perez has removed the capital C and D found in the original feeder layout

It was actually not a big move. It turned out to be significant, but that was not the publishers' and/or the writer's intention in 1828. They could not have imagined and were not thinking that the entire future, and thus history, of one of the most popular games of all time would be influenced by this simple adjustment. Very simple.

Yet, as mentioned, the entry in the book gets reprinted, copied, and repeated word-for-word in many books after this entry.

Though it had an enormous impact, it was not a big crime: The publishers were just trying to serve the US publishers, their agreement, and the book's target market or audience—youth playing ball in Boston, New York City, and other US cities.

It Is Not a History Question. It Is a Marketing Question

It is about the business of publishing; what they must do to be profitable. Publishers look for content that will appeal to their specific marketplace. The London publishers would have wanted a candidate that was similar to what the publishers in Boston and New York were asking for, and rounders was a perfect candidate because, frankly, it actually was not that popular. By their mention of feeder, they were free to adapt the less popular rounders to their purpose.

Henry Chadwick Said Rounders Was . . . Well . . . Round

Henry Chadwick, a key early figure in establishing baseball as a popular sport in the United States, apparently played rounders as a boy in England and said the game had a round base layout. To set up the rounders layout, he said, one needed to do the following:

> . . . dig a hole in the ground for the home position, and place four stones in a circle, or nearly so, for the bases.[32]

Basically rounders, he states, had five bases to form somewhat of a circle. So it was "very similar" to feeder.

But for the record, stones are not baseball "bases," and other mentions tell of rounders using sticks; townball definitely used sticks in the ground. Also, a *hole in the ground* is not a home plate. In some of these games, you could get the batter out by getting the ball back to home and plugging it (placing it) down into the hole, after a hit.

Chadwick was born in Exeter, which is located in the southwest of England—wow—and that makes his connection to the round-shaped rounders base layouts rather credible. Did Chadwick suggest he felt rounders was the source of baseball? Yes.

Though Chadwick was from England, he was four years old when the first edition of *The Boy's Own Book* was released and he was 13 years old when his family moved to the United States. So he would have naturally seen similarities between baseball in the United States and rounders in his home country. So any imaginary juror reading the statement above should keep a boy's bias, and fond childhood memories, in mind when looking at baseball's origin. But for now, we are not looking at the "bases" used in rounders but the "base" layout. Chadwick basically said it had five and that the layout was round. But hold on. Wait a minute!

On second reading, do you understand what game Chadwick is really talking about here? Feeder. Of course he was! His description matches the descriptions of feeder found in *The Boy's Own Book* which emphatically goes out of its way to state feeder was the game played in places like Exeter—Chadwick's hometown.

By the time of his statement, Chadwick was looking back at history through a prism, at a time when rounders was considered the go-to candidate. Remember rounders and feeder were "very similar." But the truth is, neither was actually similar to baseball.

Great but Human

In his 1888 book titled "Base-ball: How to Become a Player,[33]" John Montgomery Ward identifies three issues impacting baseball origin history. But first, keep in mind that the period he is writing about was not long after the US declared independence from England. Here is how Ward explains it:

"There were then, as now, persons who believed that everything good and beautiful in the world must be of English origin, and these at once felt the need of a pedigree for the new game. Some one of them discovered that in certain features it resembled an English game called "rounders," and immediately it was announced to the American public that base-ball was only the English game transposed."

Second, Ward highlights a major pitfall impacting documentation around baseball's history—in this case, biased articles and publications promoting an agenda: "This theory was not admitted by the followers of the new game, but, unfortunately, they were not in a position to emphasize the denial."

Third, despite his clear admiration for the Englishman driving the theory, Ward goes on to explain why the Englishman was driving it and how he was driving it: "One of the strongest advocates of the rounder theory, an Englishman-born himself, was the writer for out-door sports on the principal metropolitan publications. In this capacity and as the author of a number of independent works of his own, and the writer of the "base-ball" articles in several encyclopedias and books of sport, he has lost no opportunity to advance his pet theory."

Out of respect, Ward doesn't mention him by name, but it is clear whom he means. Ward even praises him, saying that he himself "entertains the greatest respect for that gentleman, both as a journalist and man, and believes that base-ball owes to him a monument of gratitude." That could only describe and be one man: Henry Chadwick. Chadwick, often called the father of baseball, is great. But he is also human. Ward's comments strongly suggest the notion that baseball was born in England was agenda-driven and a pet theory—but not the truth.

Dead in the Water: Rounders Loses the Diamond Shape

Even if you reject everything I have written so far, here is the killer piece of evidence which is what I might use in a closing argument if this were a courtroom: The key evidence that proves rounders was not diamond-shaped comes from the very same book: *The Boy's Own Book*. That evidence is from editions starting around 1849 and after.

That is right. In later editions of *The Boy's Own Book*, the London publishers revamped the base layout design of rounders away from a diamond shape. It was probably at a point in time when book sales had declined. In fact, it was actually the first shape that I found for rounders in the spring of 2020. So, later, when I came across that diamond shape, I went back and rediscovered that David Block also states in his book *Baseball Before We Knew It* that the description of rounders' "reverted" in later editions, such as one in 1849.

Wow. That was confirmation for me and a great relief. But in doing the footnotes for this second edition, I had to go back and find David's actual statement, and in doing that, I found even more evidence. Here is that paragraph from Block's *Baseball Before We Knew It*:

> **In at least one later English edition (1849), the shape of the playing field reverted from a four-base diamond to a five-base pentagon configuration, while the American editions continued to describe rounders with four bases.**

You mean the diamond shape is replaced by a box-and-one shape or pentagon shape? Let me present this as a highly technical question: *Excuse me?!!*

And why did the publishers change the London version but not the US version? The reason is that the US publishers knew that popular US city games used a diamond-shape, but the London publisher knew the layout of rounders in England was *not* diamond-shaped.

As added evidence, if you research the many old descriptions of rounders, you will find that rounders had, not one, but various base layouts: round, box-and-one, pentagonal, and even rectangular.

One note: That is a reason it took me months to understand all of this—the first shape I saw was that box-and-one shape for rounders. Then I saw a pentagon shape. All these various descriptions of it's layout had me scratching my head when I found the diamond shape in that 1828 second edition. I was even frightened at first since it was a few months into my research—I felt that I had made a big mistake. As I came across conflicting research and statements—my baseball concept model gave me the confidence to challenge things and dig deeper. Without it, I would have left most of it at face value.

Did We Miss This *Strike* As Well?

The 1828 second edition of *The Boy's Own Book* also states that in rounders if a player "misses three times" that player is out, yet in the later, 1849, edition, it reads that "the in-player is also out if he miss striking the ball." In other words, the player is only allowed one miss, not three. So let me use another, but this time, ancient philosophical question: *Say what, bro?!!*

That is the opposite of what it should be; it represents a regression in the sport. It would be like basketball starting its own history with only the three-point play and then many years later adding the two-point play while losing that three-point play. In terms of the progression of the sport, it makes zero sense. It is not only illogical but impossible. Here is what that means:

To believe that rounders actually had a diamond shape is to believe that rounders is the only sport—IN HISTORY—that regresses over time. It goes backward, gets less organized, over time. And that is crazy!

We go from a diamond shape in 1828 to a box-and-one shape (or pentagon-like shape) in 1849, meaning a shape where the "feeder" throws a ball underhand to a player who is actually positioned between what for us would be first base and home plate.

Just as damaging, that 1849 description also mentioned *one* miss, not *three* missed swings, allowed. New York Base-Ball Club member, John Montgomery Ward confirms this only *one* miss allowed rule for rounders in his book, *Base-ball: How to Become a Player,* (Philadephia: The Athletic Publishing Company), 1888.

The progression of the game toward the perfection we find in the diamond shape doesn't happen. It goes backward. It would be like football suddenly getting rid of, or disallowing, the forward pass two years from today. Would you get rid of the three-point play in basketball? Rounders goes backward, gets less organized, less perfected. It regresses.

So What Else Does This Suggest If Not Prove?

That description suggests that the 1828 second edition of *The Boy's Own Book* may become very important once again, but for the opposite reason.

US publishers had to get permission to republish the book in the US. It was most likely the US publishers who influenced the London publishers' decision to use a diamond-shaped layout in the description of a book going to the US. That means that the diamond shape was already found here in the US.

Even though there is still more evidence to come, when the circumstantial and direct evidence around rounders is considered, it suggests beyond a reasonable doubt that baseball, American baseball, actually comes from the United States because the diamond shape within the rounders description could only come from one place: the United States.

Amazingly, instead of proving rounders was the origin of American baseball, that rounders entry in the second edition, published in 1828, shows that bat-and-ball games from the United States were the actual critical inspiration for the contrived 1828 entry—yes, the very one used to prove baseball comes from Britain. This destined-to-be-infamous 1828 entry can now be used to prove that there was a diamond-shaped layout in some bat-and-ball game being played in cities such as New York and/or Boston.

To be clear, this coming statement does not apply to some vague, obscure game also called "rounders" out there somewhere in the countryside in the west of England around 1828—its existence is possible and probable. This statement applies to a different, or false, "rounders" as found in that 1828 entry:

It was US bat-and-ball games—most likely stickball—coming from cities like New York that were the origin of *rounders* and NOT the other way around. That 1828 "rounders" entry, the one used to prove baseball originated from England, proves the exact opposite—it proves that the US is the origin of that false "rounders." Now that is a new historical twist. Ironically, perhaps the name *rounders* is perfect. The whole thing went *round* and *round*—meaning instead of coming from England to the US, it went from the US over to England then *round-back* to the US. That 1828 entry—as false advertising—proves baseball, our baseball, originated in the US.

It is important to note that the book was intended for youths; that points to street games played in city streets or open lots close to where these youths lived. That bigger New York City geometry would have encouraged a diamond shape—and rounders, by the book's own first description, was played where? In the countryside.

So next, how do we knowingly and essentially define what it is we call baseball? We have to turn to the abstract nature of the sport, not just the physical.

If you are using the physical, you indeed go back to prehistory. And we will always be finding another *Ts'u-chü* (Cuju-like) game, played with a *ball* back in China around 2500 BC —a ball back then is already half of any bat-and-ball game. Or even the bat-and-ball game that came from ancient Egypt called *seker-hemat,* which translates to *"batting the ball."* Apparently they played it as far back as 2400 B.C., according to Egyptologist Peter A. Piccione, Ph.D. There is even a wall relief dated c. 1460 from Pharaoh Thutmose III's rule showing that game.

Just to note it, in rounders the players run counterclockwise around the "base" layout, not clockwise. After hitting the ball, they would head to what for us would be third base. To me, the counter-clockwise set up speaks to rounders lacking something in its competitive nature.

In the end, it is simple logic: It's called rounders as in *round*.

CHAPTER ELEVEN

TAG THIS—THE
ORIGIN
OF ALL OF IT

I'm going to write about the origin of it all. By that I mean the origin of key elements—not the actual birth of baseball as a professional sport. Perhaps some of you will want to toss this out. "Are you actually going to talk about *tag*?"

But stop. Think differently.

Look at it from an essence or concept point of view, which involves a logical deconstruction of the essence of where these elements come from. Once deconstructed, we can use that deconstructed essence as yet another guide. We can then use this exercise to gain a deeper understanding of real baseball (not just the pretenders) and baseball's real origin.

It's the Abbott and Costello lesson. What are we looking for? Are we just looking for the word *baseball* in some book, or some document, or some proclamation? Or are we looking for the essence of baseball as found in baseball itself?

Regardless of the name, the time, or the place, here's where all of those games and sports come from. All of them.

I will present it as a list; then go through each one.

1. Tag, you're it.
2. You're safe.
3. A reason to be unsafe.
4. Caveman teenagers.
5. Bat and ball origin.
6. Geometry and numbers.

So let's start to go through that list—or our lineup.

1. Tag, You're it

Tag is the origin of all of it.

Kids play tag. They don't have to read a book on it. It doesn't have to be handed down. They just do it. All kids play. All sophisticated animals play. It's also spectacularly important to animal survival. That's where they develop the skills needed to survive. Most likely, it's really critical for us as well.

Does anyone reading this think that kids in the Roman Empire or the Egyptian Empire did not play tag? Of course they did. Things are true whether written down or not. It's simple human nature.

2. Safe

If you played tag for even five minutes as a kid, you already know this: It's exhausting. Especially if it's nonstop. So kids need a rest, a safe place, perhaps a tree or a stump. Or some column perhaps? A pedestal of some kind? Or later, the side of a home. Anything he or she can touch and claim as a safe spot.

3. A Reason to Be Unsafe

Now as a one-time-kid, you know that once you are on that base or that safe spot, you're not going to get off it. Nobody does. That always becomes the end of the game. Right? "OK, well, if you're not going to step away from that base, I'm out of here. I'm going to do something else, like maybe *beat the crap out of you* for not getting off the base!"

So they had to devise something to get the kid off the safe base. How about a second base? How about something that makes the kid go to the other base, like getting a point? How about a ball knocking down one of the bases so the kid or player had to go to the other base? How about one player using a bat to prevent the other player from knocking down the safe base, so the player didn't have to run to the next base?

I don't know. But the simplicity is this—the numbers expand. One, two, three, four, five, and it keeps going—and it did. The game described in 1796—some refer to it as English base-ball— in a book written by Johann Christoph Friedrich Guthsmuth,[34] technically had six or seven bases when you include its "home plate"—which was actually a zone (defined as A-to-B). To our point, apparently that game always descends into a mass *tag* game. One team versus the other. How do we know? It is actually in the rules. Apparently, it was the part that Guthsmuth himself loved about the game.

4. Caveman Teenagers

It is what I call a question. Let me ask you to think about it. Did cavemen and cavewomen have teenagers? Yes, they did.

And they were not idiots. Rocks, pedestals, sticks, balls—all of those things were there. And if you were a kid and you had something round and a stick around—they had those, of course—at some point in time you're going to play a bat and ball kind of game. Even using your hand as a bat, right?

Of course they did. That's human nature.

So just imagine if you're a five-foot caveman or cavewoman and you're reaching for an apple or some fruit that is eight feet high, and you have a stick. You're going to do what? Bat it down!

And if your teenage son or brother is around, he'll probably find some fruit lying on the ground and throw it your way; and you're probably going to hit it. Or at least try. It's just human nature. It's like swimming. If there is some water around, people are going to jump in it and try swimming.

And keep this in mind: Apparently, we are so smart today that it is assumed everybody in prerecorded history was stupid, right? Want proof? Geico made a fortune off of commercials of cavemen upset they were treated like idiots. We all remember those ads.

Cavemen and cavewomen had teenagers and kids that played. Well, what did they play with? Anything they had around. What would you do if you saw a rock? You would pick it up and throw it. Hopefully not at someone but at something. How about a rock on top of another rock on top of another rock that you were trying to knock down. In other words, how about throwing a rock at a pedestal? Of course they did that.

Rocks were used by cavemen and cavewomen to do stuff. One of those things was to defend themselves. So you can imagine that throwing a rock accurately might be a good thing. It was probably encouraged or taught to them by their fathers or mothers.

But what do you throw at? You throw it at a tree, a tree stump—a target of some kind. Or you build a target, like a pedestal, which at that time was probably a group of rocks set up to look like a pyramid. The fact is that they threw it at whatever they decided to throw it at.

5. Bat and Ball Origin

Bat-and-ball is too broad a category. And let me just add this:

I feel guilty writing the obvious, but there are so many people who have used the bat-and-ball thing to prove another bat-and-ball thing was the source of baseball. No. I don't know if you get the sense of it, but you could make that argument. But for me, it's just superficial at best.

Are there some influences there? I don't want to give anyone that because it's foundationally based on too broad a reasoning, which would not allow for unrelated developments.

Look, no one invented rock-throwing although pitching was developed—you could say—from that. But not really. It's like saying that some document is the first to record a man or a woman throwing a rock. Does it mean that the source of Major League Baseball is from that person? I don't think so.

And now you see why I had to use *the obvious* to get to what isn't obvious.

In the end, it's all obvious.

6. Geometry and Numbers

What is *four bases* in baseball? It is a shape. Break it down to its essence, and it's also a number:

> **One**—Tag. You need a home place. That is the number one.
> **Two**—Cricket. You have two bases—a reason to leave one safe spot and go to the next.
> **Three**—Like *three-corner* or *three old cat*. Cat was more like a regiment. And there was *one, two, three*, and even *four old cat*. (with basically a catcher and thrower at each corner)
> **Four**—Well, we go back to our core concept: Numbers one, two, and three. What's next? Simply the number four.

Also, rounders and some others of these early games, if Chadwick is correct, sometimes could have as many as eight bases or even more. That suggests these "bases" were more like markers.

But now think of growing US cities, like a sprawling New York City in the late 1700s and early 1800s. The layout or geometry of its streets would suggest a progression—empty lots disappearing, or good playing fields being pushed further and further away, and more and more pick-up games being played in the streets—moving the game play towards a specific base layout influenced by all that.

Like these cities themselves, the games youth played were developing. Think of it in light of math. You start with one base, but it is actually two because of home base. Then perhaps a triangle as you cut across a street to reach *second* base, then ultimately settling on *four*—a diamond shape. Why diamond shape? Because if you were in the middle of the street, you were not going to make first base only ten feet away, to your right. It would not work as a boxed shape. So, logically, in the heart of progressively bigger and bigger US cities (with wider streets), a diamond shape would become the natural end of a progression from one to two to three to four bases used in something like stickball.

Remember, by its own description in 1828, rounders was played in the country, not in the city. If you are in wide open spaces, a wide-open field, the first thing that comes into your mind is not a diamond shape layout or field. It's much more natural for the countryside to suggest a rounder shape, thus the name rounders.

So, I clearly state for the record, a concept modeling, essence-based analysis of American baseball suggests, in reality, baseball did not come from rounders, townball, stoolball, tut-ball, trap-ball, or English base-ball, or from *A Little Pretty Pocket-Book*, or even the Tudor dynasty.

So where did American baseball come from? Its name, and everything else, comes from—what? That is next.

Part III

CHAPTER TWELVE

THE TWIST IN WHERE
AMERICAN BASEBALL
REALLY COMES FROM

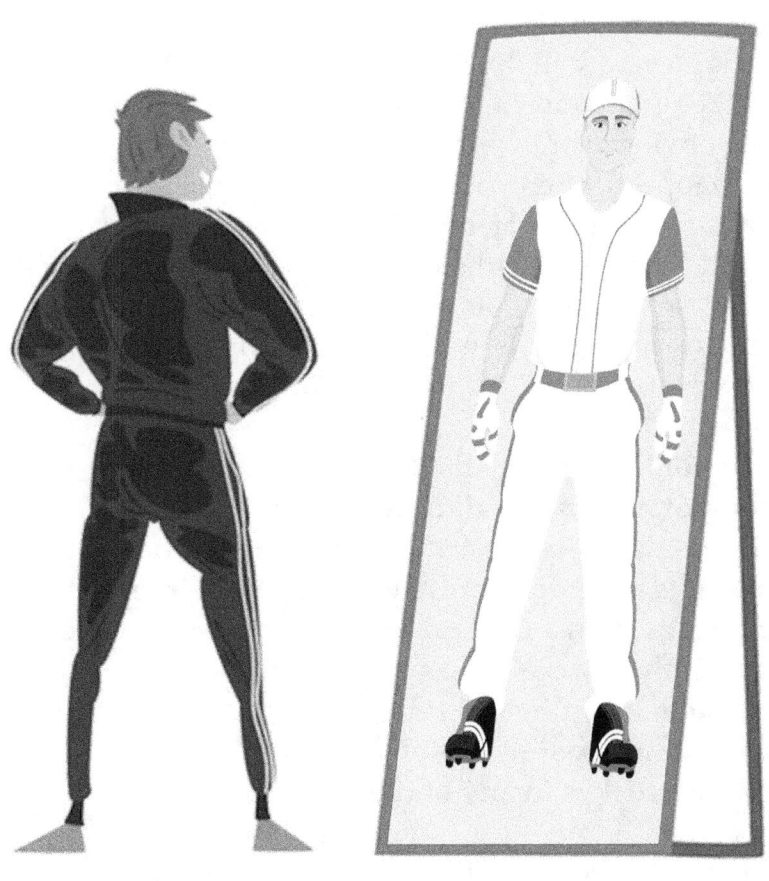

Heads up—an obvious reminder: Bat and ball are the core stuff baseball is made of. Those two things drive everything else in the sport. Simple. Perhaps as simple as it gets.

But that's not the heads-up. There are going to be many times as you read this book, that you will feel the tug of the obvious. Your brain will shout out, "Yeah, I already know that!" Then you will feel a mental impulse to skip over it, or stop reading. What you may not know is that reaction is built into us. It is indeed evolutionary—if we didn't skip past obvious things, our brain would go on overload. Enough said—its a topic for another time and from my concept book.

But here is the truth. Essence always turns out to be obvious. So by going in and through what feels too obvious, we can get to new and deeper insights on the essence of something we thought we knew. In our case, within this book, we will discover insights that prove baseball's true origin.

In this chapter we will dive head first into things that are not obvious at all. Yet in an amazing twist, these too will become obvious shortly—the obvious isn't.

So what happens when you set the physical aside and delve into baseball's abstract nature? Here is the conclusion you are left with:

None of the claimants to the throne of being the origin of American baseball carry the concepts at the core of the sport. ***None!***

Believe it or not, here is what all these pretenders and all the games that came before 1828 did not have:

They did not have baseballs. Period.
They did not have baseball bats. Period.
They did not have bases. And, as mentioned, that is one of the key ones. It is so important we will step back into that for some other findings from a concept model of a base. None of these games actually had bases—as in baseball bases.
None of them had gloves.
Pitching did not exist in any of these games.
They had no strikes in any of these games.

If you don't believe it, the trick is to dig deeper and ask yourself this: What is a *bat* exactly? Beyond some obvious, superficial things, how is it truly different from a stick? Before concept modeling a bat,

I did not know. I thought I knew, and I knew it up to a point, but I didn't know. Why? Because the answers to those questions go beyond the physical. The ultimate answers stem from concept, and concept is layered—it keeps going and going and going.

To prove that, let's go to a different, even deeper layer within our baseball—the thing that makes it American.

None of these sports had the attitude, the athleticism, the competition, the organization, or the inherent American spirit found in American baseball. It is just not there.

In other words, if you look at baseball as a competitive, athletic sport that turned into what it is today—a major sport and a successful business—none of that was there.

For the record, let's review specific pretenders. As shown, rounders is not the source of baseball. English base-ball—is not the source of baseball. Cricket is the one that comes close, but it is entirely different sport altogether—it is not the source of baseball. Tut-ball—is not the source of baseball. German ball, longball, poison ball—which is the French version—stoolball, and all of these and so many, many others are not the source of American baseball.

So what does the sheer number of contenders tell us?

If you have dozens of contenders, then you actually have no contenders. What do I mean by that? It tells you more about, not the contenders, but the nature of bat-and-ball itself. That nature has to do with a spontaneous ability to appear anywhere in history, any time in history, and any place in history. If there is a bat and ball around, people are going to play with them.

But here is the key question: If every country has pretty much demonstrated a rather independent tendency, if not spontaneous ability, to launch some kind of bat-and-ball game, why should the USA be any different? It's not.

It is like water. If there is water around, people are going to jump in it. And if you think of a bat as a stick, you go back to prehistory for sure.

The Physical Versus Baseball's Deeper Nature

Bat, ball, and base. These are all physical things. It is simple. But there is a caveat. The abstract nature of those things—the sheer number of concepts involved—is actually surprisingly complex.

For example, baseball involves *activities* such as pitching, batting, and base stealing. A *bat* is different in nature from pitching. Yet both involve concept. And that has implications on how we deconstruct and understand them.

Did you ever consider the nature of *activity* itself? Activity is, once again, one of those obvious things. We all know—in fact, we know it instantly—what base stealing is. But as we discussed in chapter five, base stealing has a nature and structure to it. We learned that base stealing joins an activity with a physical thing. The activity of *running* is married to a physical thing—a *base*.

Now stop. Stop. Forget everything—absolutely everything you understood about it as a physical activity. Try to go past the obvious and see it in a new light. The abstract essence of it. In simple terms, the abstract is somehow glued to the physical. It is a bit like permanently gluing a cloud to a flagpole. We are so used to seeing base stealing as an activity that we skip right by the extraordinary nature of what that means.

You can glue a physical baseball to a physical glove—perhaps right into the pocket of the glove. But how do you glue an activity to a base? As we discussed, that skill—meaning base stealing as a concept and an activity—is unique to baseball.

Obviously, you can touch a bat or a ball, but you cannot touch a "pitching"; you can only touch someone who is pitching. Again, you cannot touch a pitch, you can only touch a thing that is being pitched, like a ball or, hopefully, your future spouse when you pop the question!

It is a different way to think about the nature of reality—you think about it from a concept modeling point of view. In concept modeling, an *activity* is a concept. *Activity* also is part of concept modeling's definition of concept itself. All that has to do with the true nature of the abstract world itself. (For reference purposes, a new definition of concept can be found in my book *Concerning the Nature and Structure of Concept*. And just to note it, according to that book, the current definitions of concept are wrong.) Throughout human history, there's been confusion about the difference between idea and concept—but that discussion is for another time. So here is the short and the obvious of it applied to baseball and this book:

There are concept layers within those physical things that define their essence and that of the sport itself; there is a clear distinction in the layers that make baseball, baseball. The deeper you dig, the more you can separate and distinguish US baseball from any other game before it. And there are ten-times-ten as many abstract concepts that make baseball, baseball than there are physical things that make the sport what it is.

Why is that important? We can use the hidden concepts to prove baseball comes from the United States while we learn to see deeper into this beloved sport. So we are going to briefly start with the physical things we have already touched upon, then go into the physical things we have not touched upon, and then go into the abstract things, most of them activities, that make baseball distinct. Using concept models, we will deconstruct those specific and unique activities. Finally, we will explore some even deeper concepts found in American baseball. Oh yeah. Even deeper!

To help give us a framework, there are four points to keep in mind:

Point One: American baseball comes from baseball things that are *made in America*. Not Europe.

Point Two: American baseball also comes from American stickball.

Point Three: American baseball comes from American baseball. And there is a twist to that statement which we will address shortly.

Point Four: There is a reason we don't officially call it American baseball, yet we still call it America's game.

We will go through those by looking at concept models on specific physical things and activities that make baseball, baseball—and that make baseball almost the perfect sport, and often spectacular.

CHAPTER THIRTEEN
GLOVES: USA 1—EUROPE 0

The Obvious Isn't...in Baseball

Baseball Glove Concept Model

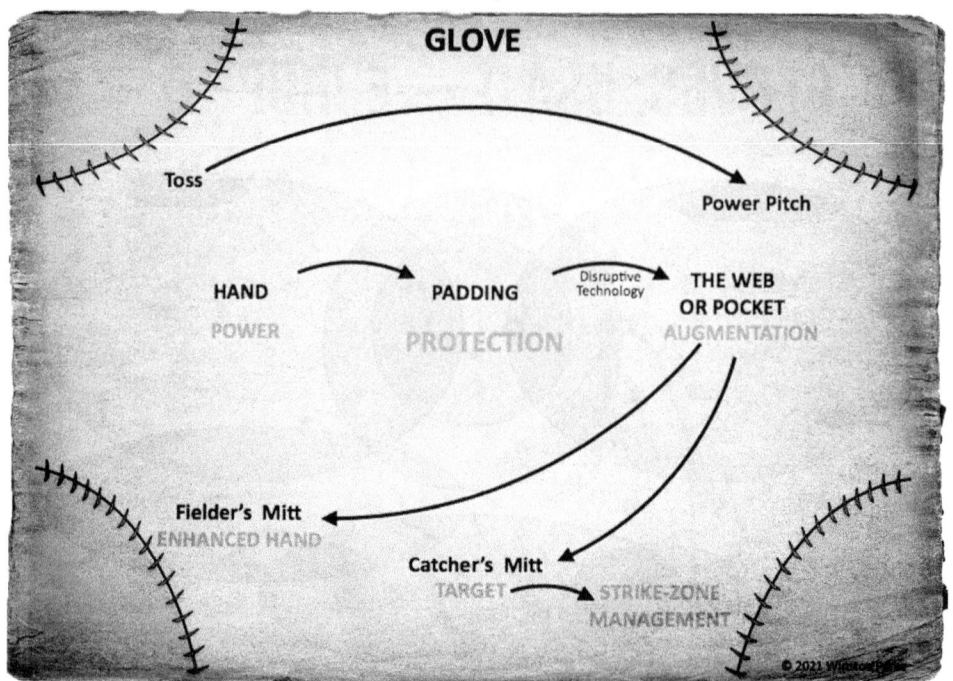

Fig. 22: Baseball Glove Concept Model by Winston J Perez   Copyright 2022 Winston J Perez

Gloves: USA 1—Europe 0

In the fifth chapter, we talked about gloves in detail. The first glove came into the sport in 1874 and the first truly modern glove came in 1919 or 1920. Baseball gloves come from America. They were truly American made.

Rounders. Townball. Tut-ball. Stoolball. None of them used gloves. It was the change in how the ball was tossed, then later pitched to a player in the game played in the US, that made the creation of the first real baseball glove inevitable.

Author's Note: The lighter text within these concept models is designed to reveal the deeper but hidden layers of concepts within the models. Like true abstract concepts, they are always there but not that easy to see.

CHAPTER FOURTEEN
BASES: USA 2——EUROPE 0

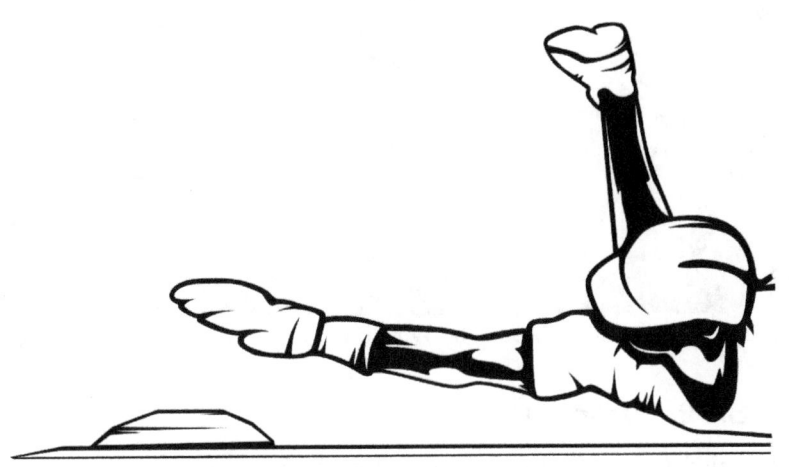

Baseball Base Concept Model

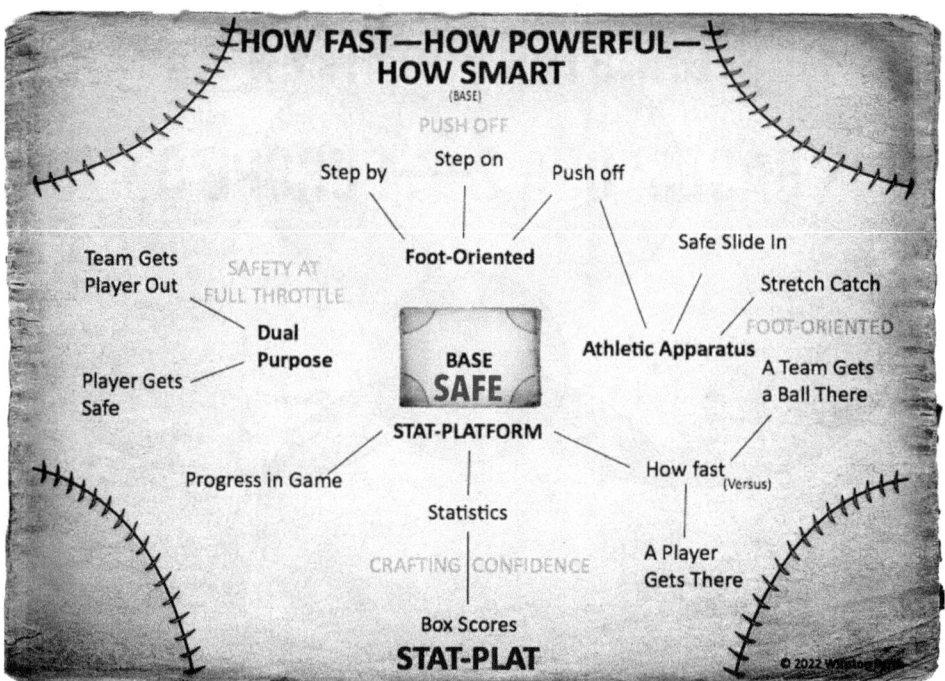

Fig. 23: Baseball Base Concept Model, by Winston J Perez   Copyright 2022 Winston J Perez

Bases: USA 2–Europe 0

In chapter eight we discussed this. A stick in the ground is not a base.

But I want to add one other distinguishing feature into the mix. In those early games, you were not out if someone threw the ball to another team player touching what for us would be first base; in other words, no one was called out with a "first base" player catching the ball and tagging, not the runner, but the base. So that again means it was not a base as in an American baseball base. Not close!

In chapter eight, we mentioned that a base is a stat-plat. But what the heck is a stat-plat? Above is a concept model on a *base* to help explain it.

A base is not a stick in the ground—as in townball or rounders. It is also not three sticks in the ground, as found in cricket. A base is not a marker—one that you run past, around, or use to outline part of a circuit. As developed in the United States, a base is also more than a bag filled with sand, or a canvas or rubberized square that is

15 inches by 15 inches. It is any one of those things, but it is also what I call a stat-plat, which is short for a Stat Platform.

A base is what establishes the fourth significant stat in baseball. First you have a pitch—its kind, speed, and accuracy. Second, you have the batter result—he connects with the ball or not. Then you have either a fly ball caught for an out, or as a second choice, you have a ground ball, a hit—meaning the batter goes to at least first base safely.

Stat

Here is the oddly obvious thing. It is something we don't think about in depth. What establishes a hit? First base does that. In other words, if a batter just strikes the ball, it is not a hit until it relates to first base and/or other bases. Think of it this way: Is it a hit if a batter hits a foul ball? No. Getting to first base or beyond counts as a hit. Is it a hit if a batter hits a fly ball that is caught? No first base—no hit. What if a batter hits a home run? He gets to go past first base and around the circuit to home plate. The definition of a home run directly involves a base. This is the definition of a home run taken from *Merriam-Webster's* online dictionary (retrieved 4/26/2022): "a hit in baseball that enables the batter to make a complete circuit of the bases and score a run." No bases? No home run.

First base is about a stat. It is literally a platform for stats.

Did you make it to first safely or not? Its distance and required positioning is critical to the game. A player must make it to first base, which is 90 feet from home plate. That 90 feet establishes the competitive nature of the sport. It is not a game, but a sport. The 90 feet injects the sport with another number; it is yet another reason or proof baseball is a numbers game. Imagine a base ten or twenty feet from home, (like some early European games) and you get the picture. It is located at the perfect distance. Too short and everyone is safe. Too long and no one is safe unless there's a home run, which is what some early European games were all about; you had markers—sticks or sometimes brickbat—and you either made it around the entire circuit without being hit with the ball or you did not.

As mentioned in chapter six, the 90 feet as a number is one of many things that proves that it was numbers that established the essence of the game, unlike almost any other team sport. By that

I mean there is no fudging that distance, much the same way the 100-meter race in the Olympics is defined by that 100 meters. More than would be the case for a box or circle, the construction of an accurate diamond layout is driven by numbers.

Platform

If you look at our Baseball Base Concept Model above, it is amazingly complex for what started in America as just a bag filled with sand. Yet look at all the elements that come out of this simple thing. It's amazing. It was completely unexpected until I did the concept model.

The personal lesson for me in deconstructing the essence of baseball was the unexpected fact that I kept learning something new every day by concept modeling even the most basic of elements/equipment/tools used within the sport, looking for the essence of those things. The structure of essence involves concept, and concept comes in layer after layer after layer.

One of the things you can find within the model is the concept of a platform. A base is a functional piece of equipment within the sport of baseball that delivers several functionalities. In other words, it is a platform because it has various specific and distinct uses. You could contrast that with a bat, which has one and only one function: A bat is used to hit a baseball. Period.

The simplest example of how the platform concept translates or how you can see its nature as a platform lies in its multiple purposes: For example, a player needs to be able to safely slide into the base either by foot or by diving and stretching out and down, extending hands first. In those circumstances, the base as a platform delivers a functionality that maximizes the full-throttled athletic competition within the sport—meaning it allows a player to run at top speed without fear of a major injury. In the game of townball, rounders, tut-ball, stoolball, or so many other early European games, that was not possible. It also speaks to intention—the European games were more fun than competitive, more in line with games than professional sports. In townball, if you ran full speed toward and through any base, you would get injured. Attempt a slide into a base using your hands, and you end the play with a broken finger or two. A so-called *base* in townball was a stick in the ground. Not the best idea.

As a platform, a baseball base is also used like a starting block for a 100-meter track race. A player will use a base as a push-off to get the maximum jump on a run to the next base off a deep fly-ball caught by an outfielder. If a player is racing around first and heading to second off an outfield hit, the base gives him the ability to add some extra speed rounding the turn to second. That is a different use of the base altogether. But there is more to a base's functionality.

Stat-Plat

When you combine the concept of *stat* with the concept of *plat*, you get a sport versus a game—meaning you get athletic competition displayed at its ultimate team-versus-one-player-at-bat challenge.

Did you ever think about that? I didn't. We move from a one-on-one competitive challenge, if you will—one pitcher against one batter—to one-on-nine instantly. Technically, the catcher is part of the pitcher-versus-batter duel, but I think you get what I mean. (Obviously, a catcher helps get it set up and delivered by creating a target.) By the one-on-nine, I mean the competitive structure jumps to one-on-nine once a ball is hit; it is now up to the team—various combinations of players or a single player—to get the batter out.

Yeah, again, you already know all that. But is that dynamic shift in its competitive structure apparent to you? One-on-one versus one-on-nine? In an instant, that shift happens. That is part of the nature or, better, the structure of the sport, and you could use that to compare it to other sports. From a concept modeling point of view, it adds a bit of complexity and variety to the sport. A fan doesn't have to be conscious of that structural shift to enjoy the game. It simply speaks to something **hidden** within the structure of the sport.

For example, in basketball, there are times when the fans know there is suddenly a one-on-one scoring situation. You can feel it—it is as if there are no other players on the court. But baseball is unique because that one-on-one is front and center; it is the focal point and always the start of a play—even if there is a steal attempt on tap. It all launches off the moment that the batter-versus-pitcher duel begins.

From a concept modeling point of view, that is interesting, but it also hints at a massive competitive difference between the early games from Europe and the game of baseball here in the United States. With the exception of cricket, which is an entirely different sport, the European pitcher—or what they more accurately called the *feeder*—was just another player on an opposing team. There is no concentrated one-on-one situation because the feeder is not trying to get the batter out. He was simply trying to get the ball in play by letting a player hit the ball.

Now, we don't see it at first glance, but as mentioned, bases also involve critical field positioning in a baseball game. Again, in those games from Europe, the position of the base didn't matter as much as it does in American baseball. And it mattered from the beginning; using a diamond shape requires more precision in the placement of first, second, and third. It forces a look at the distances involved—basically numbers.

In fact, if you study it, what these early games from Europe might have called first base was a short distance away; that is because it was often a marker, not a base. In some games, the idea was for a player to run the entire circuit to score, rounding first and so on. When I mention a base as a stat-plat, I mean its placement was important. As we get into club play or official US baseball game play, the position of the base was relevant to the creation of stats—getting to first was an accomplishment and noteworthy. Still, even in the beginning of American baseball, it was not too hard, all due to the nature of "pitching" at that time. But once real pitching entered the game, getting to first base meant something real. Thus, it was a significant stat.

So what did we just do here? Amazingly, we developed some strong logic, if not some added proof, that the United States created its own distinct bat-and-ball game. How? By walking into and through the obvious.

Outside of cricket, the European games were not really so much about stats, except runs scored. Reaching first base was not a stat. But baseball is found in things that were foundational to baseball's inherent stat-driven structure. In American baseball, a base is truly a stat-plat.

CHAPTER FIFTEEN
BASEBALLS: USA 3——EUROPE 0

Baseball (Ball) Concept Model

Baseballs were invented here. It is easier to see once you deconstruct the nature of a baseball, which is what we started to do in chapter four. This is a reminder from the 2008 Baseball Concept Model.

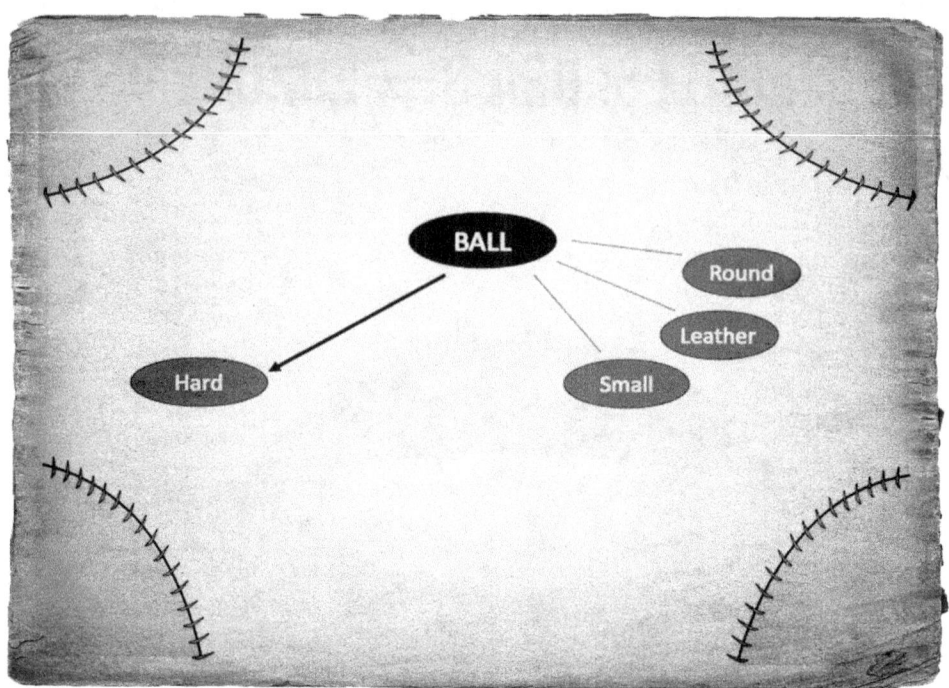

Fig. 24: Baseball Concept Model, *Concerning the Nature and Structure of Concept*, 2020, page 188

Baseball Concept Model: The Ball's Attributes

I mentioned that, suggested by my intuition way back then, I separated out the word "hard" from the other attributes. And I did that before I dug into it and found that it was an important differentiator in the games from the United States versus those from Europe.

The simple proof is that even up to townball, they threw the ball at people—that was a way they got players out. We don't allow players to throw a baseball directly at a player today in professional sports—with super athletes involved. No one is there throwing the ball trying to hit the base runner while he is running in between bases.

Imagine Aroldis Chapman doing that. Now imagine a 105-mile-an-hour throw at you as you are turning the corner to get to home plate and Chapman is determined to get you out. He'd probably break some jaws that way. You're going to be in a hospital, folks, and you're going to be pretty bruised, if not in serious trouble.

Here in the United States, that rule on getting the runner out by hitting him or her directly with the ball was changed. Worth repeating here, Wheaton mentions that was one of the first things this new competitive game would eliminate:

> **The first step we took in making baseball was to abolish the rule of throwing the ball at the runner and ordered that it should be thrown to the baseman instead, who had to touch the runner with it before he reached the base.**

If the balls used by these early European games had been like American baseballs, people would have been seriously injured at a time in history when it would have been a potentially life-threatening incident. With the exception of cricket, what some have mentioned as "hard" balls used by those European games were not that hard.

But what does Wheaton's quote tell us? It tells us that a new sport, coming from the United States, was intentionally being formed. It was harder, faster, and elevated in game play. They were creating a sport for grown-ups and athletic players who saw it as something new, more athletic, and competitive. However, the game was still not perfected; the quote suggests the use of a sand bag was relatively new because they would tag the player running to first, not just step on the base. Yet, you can see that rule change coming soon.

A full model of a baseball might actually take half this book. The official MLB rules on creating an official ball stretches to six pages alone, as we mentioned. Within our model above, those six pages would fit into just one word: manufactured. (Though it's not in this particular model.) Oh yeah, that's a book by itself.

Perhaps you have not considered something. In fact, we can do a concept experiment to draw it out: tri-ball anyone?

A Concept Experiment

Let's see what we can garner from doing one.

We wrote about round as a key attribute of a baseball. What if the ball was a different shape? What if the ball was triangle-shaped or actually a pyramid? Now you can imagine, in your mind, what a baseball reshaped into a pyramid would look like. It would still be white with red stripes going across it. You can actually visualize that.

Instead of a *hardball* it might be called a *tri-ball*. And guess what? That name works. For a professional pitcher, just imagine the wicked kind of knuckleball or other enhanced pitches he could throw using a triangular baseball. Now, imagine it from the batter's side—how hard it would be to hit a tri-ball, much less hit a home run consistently. Home runs would be incredibly more difficult to hit, if not totally dependent on luck. Possible but much, much harder. So, here's the problem, and it points to the nature of what a sport is, and that is why we did this experiment. With a tri-ball, you count on luck more than skill. And that is the difference between a game (luck predominates) and a sport.

Baseball, sometimes called the perfect sport, is perfect for displaying athleticism. It's close to perfect in that aspect.

The simplicity of a round baseball allows the pitchers, batters, and fielders to be the stars. Though at times luck is involved, baseball is a platform for a display of the grace, power, beauty, and excitement of athletic competition.

It is odd to think about. A baseball is at the center of the sport, but the sport is not actually about the baseball; it is just the means to an end. I also find it odd to express it. A basketball displays athletic skills in dribbling, passing, dunking, and shooting. In football or soccer, the ball is like a spotlight; your attention goes to wherever the ball may be found—as in carried, kicked, or passed As discussed in my book on concept, soccer has a unique concept at its core: the negation of hand use. That is what helps define the essence of that sport. Why am I writing about stuff that you already know? To change your thinking; to suggest you go beyond what is obvious to find something different—to find a deeper understanding that we tend to skip right by. It is those things that prove baseball is homegrown.

Suddenly, as I write this, I know why it is important—and I did not know why until I began writing this section. We need to ask this question: Did any of those games that were considered candidates for being the origin of baseball get the athletic nature of the game right? No, they did not.

One way to look at the distinction is the difference between a game and a sport. One could say that a game is about having fun playing it while a sport is about having an exciting time watching it. Yes, it was most likely enjoyable to watch these early bat-and-ball games, but only up to a point. It was probably not the primary reason people were there. But a sport elevates the pleasure and adds excitement to it. Sports attract real fans—people who are there for the sport itself. The perfect ball for any sport is the one that will attract fans by maximizing the athletic performance found in players with talent—often exceptional athletic talent.

So what is the point? True American baseball is not found in the ball and bat, but in a glorious sinker, a line drive and the subsequent diving catch by a shortstop, and the king of kings, the powerful home run. (We will discuss home runs shortly). So, did these European games maximize these athletic showstoppers? Did they do it in a way that drew consistent crowds? Was athleticism just an occasional sidenote, a random individual act, or was it in these European games' DNA? Was it at the core? And that is one massive difference. Baseball in the United States—by perfecting the baseball, the bases, the bats, the layout, the glove, and even the rules—perfected and even drove the athleticism within the sport.

It is part of the proof that baseball as developed in the United States was a different animal. A different breed. It was not tri-ball, dependent on luck and circumstance. It was not a game in which the perfection of the tools/instruments used were not that important. You can hear it in the Wheaton interview: He and men like him were in search of something deeper, special, and more athletic. And they injected all that into the game they created—or crafted, drawing from American bat-and-ball games, such as stickball, perhaps even *barn ball*?

One side note: In concept modeling, by doing these experiments and models and building scenarios around the obvious, we can help our minds step past the superficial and into the powerful simplicity of essence.

Our baseball was about athleticism. It was about elevating that athleticism—and that is why and how it grew. That was not the case around these European pretenders.

One fact: If you note the history of the game, once the right DNA was there, as was the case in the 1830s, and refined with the Knickerbocker Club in 1845, the game's popularity took off. The sport developed talented players and grew real fans. There was no reason these European pretenders could not have done the same thing, as was the case with cricket, which was a completely different sport. These other pretenders could have done it, but they did not. The right DNA was just not there.

CHAPTER SIXTEEN
BASEBALL BATS: USA 4——EUROPE 0

Baseball Bat Concept Model

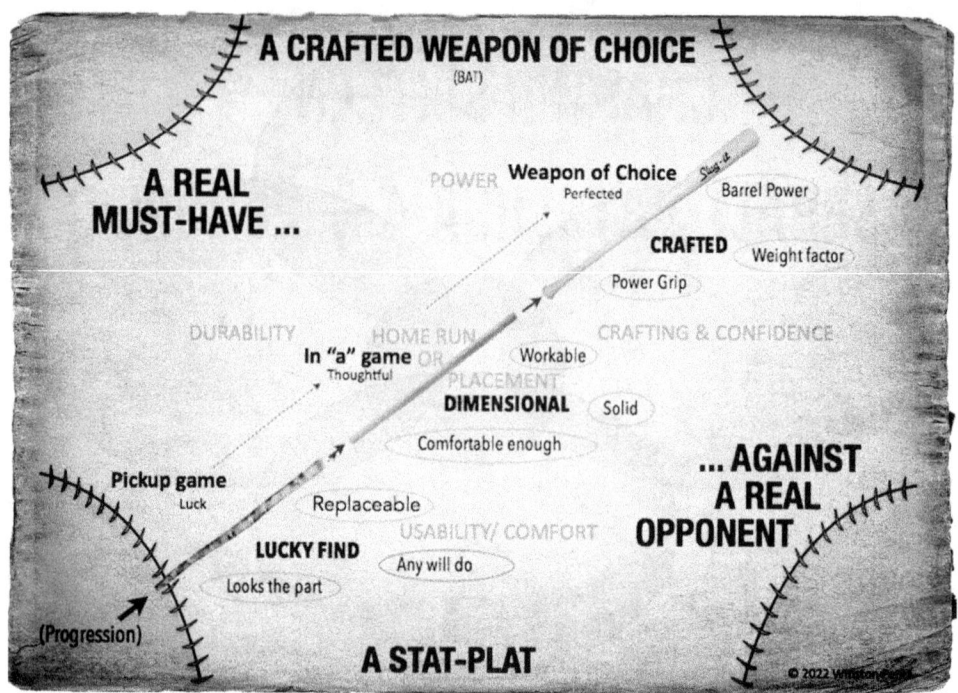

Fig. 25: Baseball Bat Concept Model by Winston J Perez   Copyright 2022 Winston J Perez

Unless you can prove to me that Europe invented sticks, baseball bats were invented here in the United States.

In 1859 you see the first official regulations on bats. In 1884 you see the first Louisville Slugger—this one handmade. Fantastic. In 1906, a baseball pitcher, manager, and soon-famous business owner, Spalding, began producing modern baseball bats in mass.

The other "bats" from Europe were more like cudgels, or they were more like the wide, flatter bats you see in cricket. Perhaps the rounders bats came from cricket. Some say they were wide bats that were shortened and made a little bit rounder. Some have stated that is the reason it's called rounders. I don't buy that. Doesn't make a lot of sense, but it could be.

A bat is not a stick, not a polished stick, not a cudgel, or wide-bat. So what is it? Let's use our concept modeling to dig down into its essence.

Concept Modeling Something As Simple As a Bat? It's Not Easy

Amazingly, of all the physical things needed to play baseball, bats were the most difficult thing for me to concept model. Just think about that for a second or two, or even three. Am I kidding? No. Why is that? Because the simplicity of a thing makes it harder to see or find anything that might break it down further. Make it more complex. Does that make sense? In other words, what else is there to discover within something as simple as a bat?

It was deceptively simple, which is probably why I didn't do a concept model on a baseball bat back in 2008. For, I assumed like most people reading this, a bat may just be too obvious to concept model.

But then I started thinking to myself, "Hey, buddy, if all this concept modeling stuff is real, you better be able to use it even on a bat!" That thought shook me a little bit. After all this work on baseball, could bat be the downfall of concept modeling and concept-based analysis? Time to step up to the plate.

Just thinking about it without concept modeling it, I could not see a way to deconstruct a bat beyond physical parts like the handle. After all, it is nothing but a polished stick, right? Yet once branded, bats made some people seriously wealthy. Hello! There has to be something more there.

The bat is one of the bigger reasons people see Europe as the origin of baseball. In documents containing drawing and illustrations, historians could see what looked like a bat. Of course, that connection relied on the illustrator's drawing skills. To my knowledge, Michelangelo never painted a bat. No still-life painter put fruits next to a bat and painted them to perfection.

Players used, well, sticks, cudgels, and fatter bats in those early games in Europe. All those things look like our baseball bat when you see the simple, old drawings. But those are not baseball bats. Period.

"What is a *bat?*" That question became my challenge in April 2022 when I was adding more material for this second edition. Ultimately, it became a forgotten lesson relearned: Trust the process—just do your concept modeling on it. But how was I going to get beyond the idea of a *stick*?

A baseball bat may be the most simple of all things baseball.

Some reading this might be thinking a ball is as simple as a bat, but that is not true: Think of the leather, the stitching, the cork and rubber core, and the wound string, and you begin to see more complexity. The model of the attributes of a baseball also suggests it is more complicated than we think.

Here is the problem with concept modeling a baseball bat: **When does a stick become a baseball bat?** That is the defining question you have to address in a concept model on a bat. That is indeed a challenge.

Starting out a little hesitant, I thought I would go up to the plate and bunt. Do a little bit of concept modeling and walk away if I got nowhere.

It was Palm Sunday, so I took a sheet of paper out and scribbled down some notes. No, I would never think about baseball during church services, would I? At least I knew it would be technically OK to think about it on the drive there. Then I would stop. No, really. For sure. Well, maybe, I might do it unintentionally for a moment or twenty-two.

The notes were OK. Just OK. Think of it like a list of things or concepts that I would have to consider and analyze as part of constructing the concept model. When it was time for church services to begin, it was an unexpected relief. I didn't have my concept modeling answer yet—on when a stick becomes a baseball bat—so this was a heavenly excuse to stop thinking about it. What can I say? I was a good boy that day for that fifty-seven minutes and thirty-three seconds!

So, I did the model the next day. And wow, sure enough, as it often happens early on in the concept modeling process, I had an intuitive feeling that came out of nowhere. I had already put the notes from the day before into the model, when suddenly that question popped back into my head:

When does a *stick* become a baseball *bat*?

I decided to get a drawing of a bat and put it next to a drawing of a stick—how simple is that, right? Very! But that is what you do in concept modeling.

You see, our mind think with words, but it also thinks with images, charts, graphs, drawings, music or sounds, and more words. So the moment I inserted a bat and a stick next to each other within the model, I knew I was missing something: A transitional "stick-bat." By that I mean something that was not just a stick, but also not yet a baseball bat. ("stick-bat" is just for concept modeling purposes.)

Here is where the model led:

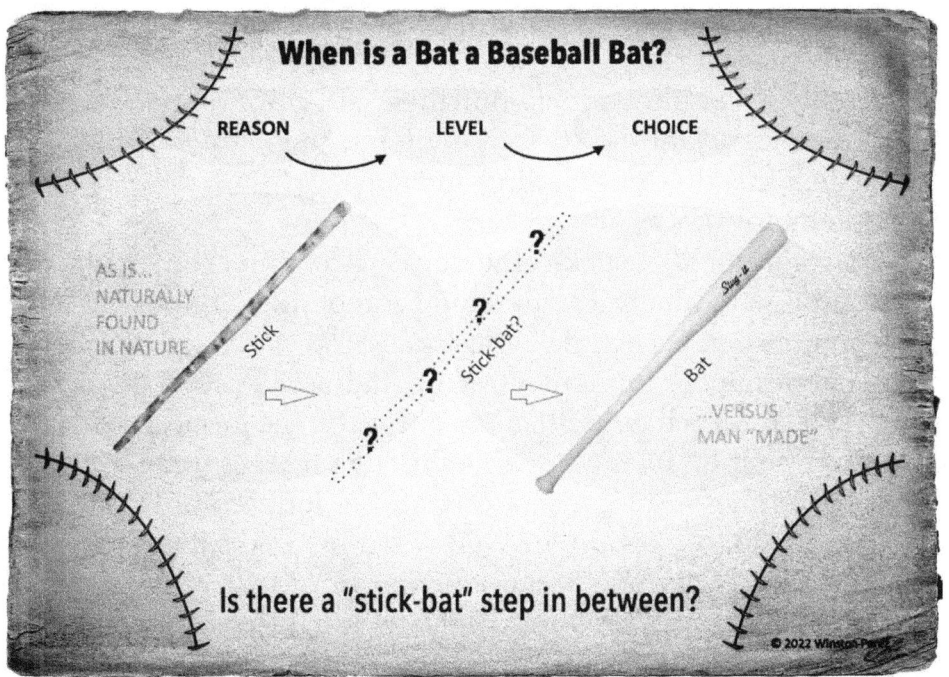

Fig. 26: Baseball Stick-Bat Concept Model by Winston J Perez Copyright 2022 Winston J Perez

Why the heck would such a simple, obvious step make a difference? Although I didn't have the answer yet, I intuitively knew that I had hit on the path that would lead me to the answer. I now felt it. I knew it. I just had to concept model it and find the discovery.

I used a storytelling experiment, which I often use in concept modeling, to help me to study it. Find it. Understand it. I developed the story to see if I could come up with something closer to the essence of a real bat.

Instantly, in the playing field of my imagination, I am time traveling in search of the earliest sticks used by humankind. And zap! I am back in prehistory as a caveman.

In my imagination, while scavenging for food for hours, I stop and eye a three-foot, sturdy-enough stick lying on the ground. I pick it up. Why? Because, a few seconds before, I had looked over to see my teenaged "cave-brother" with a rotten fruit in his hand ready to throw it at me. Soon he does, I up-and-smash it. Well, almost. I could not tell until I hit it how rotten that fruit and my brother actually were. It splatters all over me. The gooey core pit is sticking to and dangling off my left nipple. My brother laughs. I stand numb and slimed in goo. Drenched in humiliation. And I thought I had outsmarted the hairy dirtbag!

My brother's smile widens. But then, after a moment, so does mine, as I look back at the stick in my hand then at what I want to strike next—him! He stops smiling and runs.

Zap! I am now back.

Believe it or not, that stick-centered scenario unlocked my deeper understanding. Suddenly, I understood something obvious yet new.

The point is that with a stick you *"take what you can get."* Probably not a lot of crafting, or thought, goes into it. It looks pretty good; you feel it. Test it. You try it out with a tap or two on the ground. It fits the bill, so you use it on its intended victim, like fruit or your fruitcake brother. Sometimes a stick works. Sometimes it doesn't.

Does that sound too simple? Well, it led me to the concept at the core of the necessary transition in moving from stick to a real baseball bat. That concept? *Crafting*. That will break down further into *reason, level,* and *mission*. (You could think of traditional categories like *form* and *function*.)

The next evolutionary phase in development is a *crafted stick*—perhaps not specifically for ball play yet. Rather, a crafted thing initially intended for some practical use. Think of a broom handle: bad, if secretly taken from your mom or dad from that closet back at your home, but good for using as a bat that afternoon, where it will get broken—oops!—which instantly portends future troubles. What was first a broom handle, then a bat, will soon be an instrument of perhaps a just punishment. Ouch!

We can turn to the many reasons game players had for finding one already crafted or in crafting one themselves: They might want it for a Sunday, after-church, ball-play gathering. Or for a community event like an annual town celebration or park festival. Or for just after-chores play with friends on a nearby street, field, or park.

In any case, you and your friends want to play ball. And you want to bring something special and join them as someone special. You are basically looking for something that will help you hit the ball well. There are many *reasons* for crafting.

Here is the twist that I would not see until I got into modeling real American baseball bats. (And this is exactly why you have to concept model things.)

In using all of the other bat-pretenders before, it was about just hitting the ball. Players were not worried about a pitch, meaning a pitcher really pitching it with some force and speed. As we discussed, back before American baseball, a feeder or pitcher was actually just trying to help a player hit the ball. You got the player out *after* he or she hit it (if it didn't go foul).

You see, the concept model suggests that the creation of real *baseball bats* was driven by real *pitching*—with a pitcher who is now thinking, "I am going to whiz a ball past your sorry butt and send you crying home to your mommy!"

It means that the pitcher is throwing faster, even trying some new tricks like a curveball, with a ball that is harder. So now a simple stick won't work. Not even a stick that you or someone else crafted a bit. Those kinds of crafted *stick-bats* were breaking too easily against these harder, faster, and stronger pitches.

So now you are on a *mission*. You need something for this competitive war brought to you by a true opponent—a pitcher who doesn't want you to hit the ball at all. Or just hit it weakly. This new breed of pitcher is trying to strike you out intentionally. So you need a new breed of bat. And your *mission?*—to choose or craft a weapon wisely. Light. Fast. Strong. Powerful. And where is that all happening? In the United States.

Real baseball bats are *crafted weapons of choice* for facing a pitcher with strike-out intentions, suddenly transforming it all into a more elevated, competitive game.

Like bases, bats are also stat-plats—stat platforms. Whether intended consciously in the beginning or not, stats were present in the creation of elements at the heart of the sport—driven there by an elevated competitive and athletic spirit within this *crafted* sport. Did a player hit the ball foul? Did the batter swing and miss three times? Did he hit a single? Did he hit a home run? Stats would be elevated by Henry Chadwick, who would introduce the box score. He could not have done that if some of the elements were not there already.

Stats were simply inherent within the sport from the beginning because it was part of the game's DNA. With ever increasing competition, teams began to note which players were performing the best. How do you do that, if not with stats? "John hit a homerun and three singles in the game today." The same held true with bases, which, by their nature, added value to a player's getting safely to first base. As real pitching took hold, it became an accomplishment; it meant something. Thus a significant stat. That DNA also impacted the base layout. We need to measure and lay out a diamond shape—like in street ball. Only perfect in dimensions. It simply makes more sense.

From a concept modeling point of view, if the *crafted stick* isn't about stats inside a competitive game, it is not a baseball bat. Why? Because that concept determines the length, width, weight, polish, roundness, and wood type used in the thoughtful creation of a baseball bat designed to deliver a result. And in baseball, a result is a *stat*.

Players were in search of "the perfected bat"—what batters would see as their *crafted weapon of choice*. And the harder the competition fought, the stronger the bats would be crafted to fight right back. By that I also mean that with underhand pitching, some less-crafted bats worked. As real overhand pitching came into the sport officially, those didn't work anymore.

The right concept of a baseball bat is a *crafted weapon of choice* against a real hardball, fire-spitting opponent who is pitching faster and harder to beat you and your team. The pitcher is there to get you out. Your bat is a weapon to beat him.

One note: By choice, I do not mean that anything goes. The club and soon-to-be league could decide on parameters defining an official bat (regulations) based on the best possible, fair, and competitive bat to be used against an opposing competitive pitcher. But to a player, a bat is a *weapon*. Their bat is their *choice*. That *choice* is based on how it looks and feels; how it is *crafted*.

For proof you only need to look at a batter's eyes when he picks up his *crafted weapon of choice* and tests it by swinging it around or tapping it on the ground.

"Yeah. This baby will do nicely. Game on!"

The Proof Found in Official Baseball Bats Regulations

Officially speaking, the difference between an American bat and a hand-as-a-bat, a cudgel, wide bats, a stick as a bat that is any length but no more than 2.5 inches wide (as noted in *The Rules for the Massachusetts Game (Town Ball)*) has historically been driven by a real hard ball and the true nature of real baseball pitching, which does not appear in any European-like game, including townball (as played in the United States), which dies off.

Official rules on American baseball bats were not developed until a first step in 1859, a year before the time a pitcher named Jim Creighton was about to change the nature of pitching, as I will explain.

In 1859, The Professional National Association of Baseball Players Governing Committee voted in favor of the first limitation on bat size.[35]

Inherent in the concept of a real bat is the need for it to be regulated. Why? Because an official bat should service fair, sports competition. Regulations also separate the intention of these early games from Europe: Their focus was not on maximizing competition, even though individual games may have been competitive at times. It was simply not built into their intention. Cricket did build that in and it was the first to use the word *ump*, which comes from an old French word meaning "not even" or "one without equal" (from Latin *"par"* for equal). But it was not the first to use judges. Think of the Greek Olympics. Again, cricket was a different sport and once again, the fact of its existence means that the pretenders to the throne of being the origin of baseball could have built that competitive element into their games, but they didn't.

Then, this for me is the startling proof: The first real, true, and magnificent baseball bats came into the game in 1884, which was the same year that overhand pitching was officially allowed in the game. It is no coincidence that the Louisville Slugger was developed in 1884. Spalding would soon be entering the bat-making game as well.

To be clear, in 1884, for the first time, faster overhand pitching—in our concept model that means real pitching—was allowed in official baseball. In terms of baseball bats, overhand pitching meant full-force pitching, which resulted in the need for a bat that would not break given that a baseball would be moving with greater force and speed.

As all that developed, from 1860 or so to 1884, bats were breaking too easily, which is why the stronger Louisville Slugger was needed. The creation of the first Louisville Slugger in 1884 is a historical reference point that real baseball bats were made here in the United States, as a result of real baseball, when overhand pitching was officially allowed in the game. Smack that home!

CHAPTER SEVENTEEN
STRIKES: USA 5—EUROPE 0

The Concept of Strikes within Real Pitching

One note: We now want to move away from the physical objects used to play the sport to abstract things—concepts or activities—that glue the elements of the sport together.

Baseball Strike Concept Model

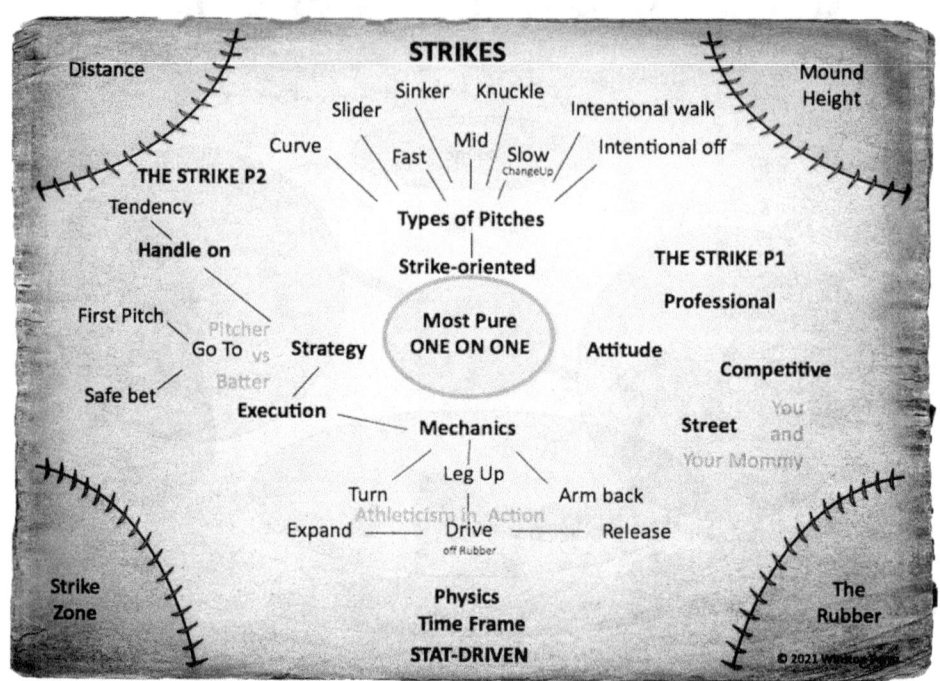

Fig. 27: Baseball Strike Concept Model by Winston J Perez Copyright 2022 Winston J Perez

I'm going to write about pitching, but I want to write about the *three-strikes* rules first because it's the easiest way to see the mistake here. Here, concept modeling steps into deconstructing the abstract nature of pitching and strikes—meaning the concepts buried deep in them that define them, separate them, and identify them as unique.

None of these contenders, and this time I'm including cricket, had baseball strikes or pitching. With regard to all these games from Europe, one of the things many historians have talked about is this: "Well, there were three misses and you're out. Three strikes and you're out." No. No. No.

There is no strike in rounders and all these pretenders. No matter what anybody tells you. This is a concept issue: In American baseball, as you all know, a strike happens when a pitcher is trying to make you swing and miss the ball. The pitcher's viewpoint is simple: *I am trying to get your butt out. I am trying to get you to miss.* With rounders, that's not the intention! Townball? That's not the intention.

It was in rounders' own rules (though, as mentioned, I believe those rules were "false advertising"). In rounders it was an *underhand, gentle* toss, folks. The fact that some players miss the ball is completely disassociated from what the pitcher throwing the underhand and gentle ball is trying to do.

That word "gentle" in the rule description is a word that describes the pitcher's intention. In rounders, it was not a strike, folks. It was simply a miss. With a miss, you're trying to have the batter hit it, so you can get him out *after* he hits it. With a strike, you are not trying to let the batter hit the ball. Two different intentions. Two different concepts.

In the beginning of townball, it was underhand as well. That would change in one region, with a different version of townball (some say a verion of a game called round ball) in Massachusetts. But even with what they called the Massachusetts Game (Town Ball), while an overhand throw was used, it was still just a throw or toss, not a baseball pitch. The intention was not about striking the batter out.

There is also a rather ginormous contradiction here: Gentle versus only three misses.

If the intention of the gentle toss was to let the players hit, then why not let them hit it by giving them a few more than three tries? In fact, why not just toss it till they hit it? Three sounds stingy when you consider it means only two more attempts after one miss. Why say, OK, here is a gentle toss right to you so you can hit it because I really want you to hit the ball, but that's it, and I am only going to give you two more times to hit it. Not three, not four, not five, only two extra. It's a bit Jekyll and Hyde, even if we are so used to three misses, when we look back historically, that we don't see the monster hidden inside there.

Why would you impose three strikes on them? More importantly, where is the logic around three when you take away the competitive nature of a pitch? If we are not so driven by competition, several more attempts wouldn't hurt. So that actually doesn't make sense.

Were they simply in a hurry? Was there a basketball playoff game on Tudor must-see TV later that night that they just had to get to their homes to watch? No. So where does that "three misses" come from? Most likely it comes from the American rules given to the London publishers for *The Boy's Own Book*, second edition, 1828 (as highlighted in chapter ten.) Of course it does, because the American game had the elevated, competitive attitude found in its game.

A Miss Versus a Strike

This is a concept issue: missing is different from a strike. Additionally, in some historically early games, if you missed once, you were out. One miss actually makes sense in some circumstances—it is not so arbitrary—where you had twenty or more people on a side.

But still, if a competitive element is entering in the game, then that's not really fair, is it? Only one chance? Because I could accidentally throw you a bad ball. So that is why you'd probably then say, "Well, you threw me a bad ball. You have to give me another shot." So you have a second shot. But you see, on the second shot, you don't really do a good job swinging. So you need a compromise, right? "You threw a bad ball the first time, and I swung badly on the second one. Let's just call it three, and we're even." That's fair play. And I think that's where the three comes from—a more competitive mindset. I'm certain of that! But people can debate that if they want to.

You might suddenly be reading this and think, *"Hey, this author is contradicting himself."* But I am not. European games were not about competition in the specific area of tossing the ball to the batter. It was just the perfect time to explain what might happen in a competitive street game where you were hoping a batter strikes out—and that is not the intention found within any of those European games, according to their own stated rules. A player simply *missed*.

All of that speaks to the counterintuitive yet common nature of concept, in that one simple addition or shift in a concept can change everything. Like circumstantial evidence examined around a crime scene, concept can alter direct evidence because concept defines essence. In the case of rounders, we mean the level or intent of the competition, or the number of players involved. In the same way, a movie character can say, "I don't like you at all" while actually meaning the opposite: "I love you."

What does all this around strikes mean in terms of baseball history? It means absolutely everything. But since the baseball *strike* obviously stems from the baseball *pitch,* I want to continue this discussion under the heading "pitching."

Next, I will be pitching a few critical proofs around the origin of baseball. So grab some peanuts and Cracker Jacks. This is where we swing for the fences. Next batter up!

CHAPTER EIGHTEEN
PITCHING: USA 6——EUROPE 0

The Obvious Isn't...in Baseball

Let me repeat it to start this section: What does all this discussion around strikes, and by extension pitching, mean in terms of baseball origin history?

What that means is that the most important pitcher of all time was Jim Creighton. Why? Creighton changed the concept underneath pitching; he was literally not a game changer but *the* game changer. Creighton was responsible for the key generational leap toward the advent of real pitching in official baseball.

One side proof of his impact was that many thought he was cheating. In other words, that is evidence that there was a real change afoot or we could say, a real change *at-hand*.

He changed the intention of a pitch even though he was doing it underhand. He was the first official baseball player to really try to strike batters out. Suddenly batters had to contend with this new thing: batting when it was no longer easy to do—when the pitcher became a new type of adversary, one who was trying to make you strike out. Could someone else have done it? Yes. But they didn't. He did it.

The Game-changer

Let me tell you, stress again, how important Jim Creighton is. He's probably the most important pitcher of all time because without him we wouldn't make that key transition.

Without him there isn't even a Babe Ruth, because what made Babe Ruth a superstar was his ability to hit those massive home runs when it wasn't easy to do because of the pitching.

Fig. 28: Conceptmodeling Baseball Card No. 3, by Winston Perez

Jim Creighton switches the direction of pitching forever. He took the first step toward a strike versus just a miss, which was different from any other official sport up to that time in history. If you are thinking about pitching found in cricket, it is completely different; in cricket, the ultimate objective of a pitcher is to knock down a bail. In American baseball, it is to strike the batter out and . . . well . . . "send you crying home to your mommy." Amazingly, that mommy quote is a critical distinction, as we will see.

In a very real way, Jim officially brought the notion of a *strike* as opposed to a *miss* into American baseball. So pitching, real pitching, comes from the United States. From a concept-based perspective, it is the most important game feature. It is literally the game-changer.

Here is a concept model on pitching:

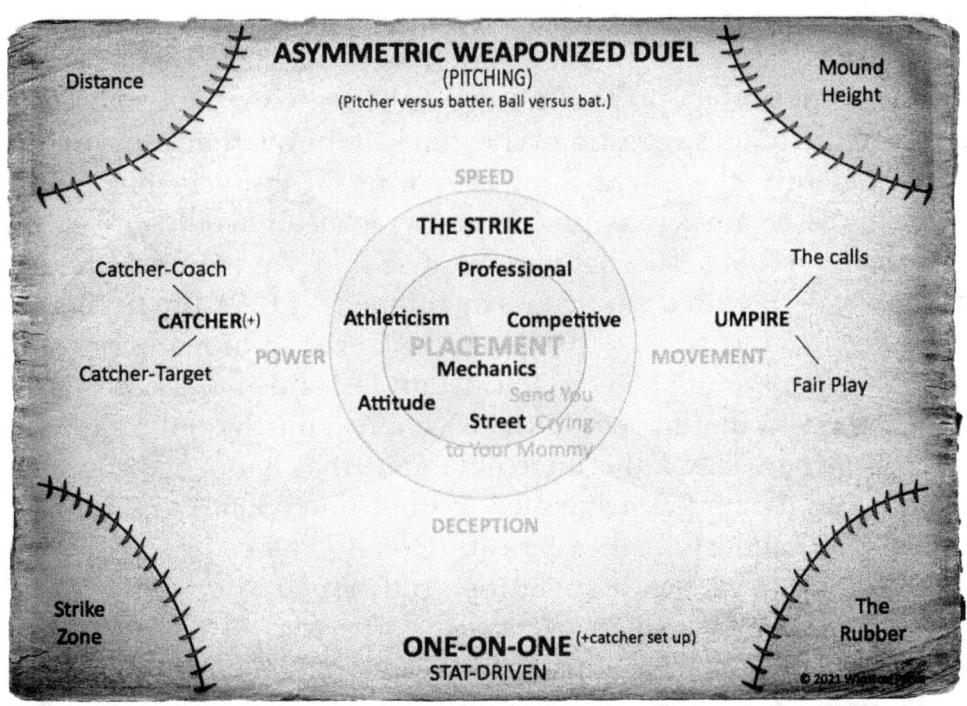

Fig. 29: Baseball Pitching Concept Model by Winston J Perez, © 2022 Winston J Perez

When you examine the concept model above, there is a lot to study there. But now try to imagine placing the rules of rounders, tut-ball, stoolball, English base-ball, or townball next to the pitching model and then comparing them. There is no strategy in an underhand toss. No types of pitches. No major mechanical movement required. In rounders it was a *gentle underhand toss*; in a later version of townball it was an *overhand throw*, but still not a pitch.

Let's go back to the interview with William Wheaton, where he makes yet another amazing statement looking back to the time they were forming this new game in New York (during the late 1830s):

The pitcher really pitched the ball and underhand throwing was forbidden. Moreover he pitched the ball so that the batsman could strike it and give some work to fielders.

Careful—it is easy to misinterpret the first line. You need the second line to get to the truth. Those lines suggest that there was no real pitching at that time in baseball history—that they started that. Again, it is the Abbott and Costello lesson. Wheaton uses the word "pitched" but that word at that time doesn't mean what we understand as *pitching* today. In the next line, he defines his use of the word: "Moreover he pitched the ball so the batsman could strike it." Folks, that is not pitching; there is no intention to strike the batsman out. That's the key. Overhand meant having more energy in a throw perhaps, but only perhaps. And the Knickerbocker Club chose underhand pitching, suggesting Wheaton lost the overhand argument.

Apparently, there was a lot of scoring in the very beginning. Some of these games were decided by which team would get to thirty or forty points first. That was because they weren't intending to get anyone out with the pitch. As mentioned, in 1860, Jim Creighton shifted it from tossing or throwing it underhand to really pitching the ball, even though he was doing it underhand.

That meant that the emphasis was not so much on the batter as on the pitcher. That's the incredible shift that happened. Because pitching, as it is today, originated in the United States in this game called baseball thirty-eight years after the first official game.

These other games from Europe did not have pitching. There was no curveball. No sliders. Those didn't arrive till at least 20 plus years after the first official game. (Guys like Candy Cummings.) So by its very own setup, rounders was never going to be American baseball. That's because in rounders the object was to give the batter the maximum opportunity to hit the ball. And the intention behind a curveball is the exact opposite. Pitching is the key. Period.

Here's the bottom line: If you are not trying to strike a gal or a guy out with a pitch that is as hard as you can throw it, it's not American baseball.

CHAPTER NINETEEN
STICKBALL: USA 7—EUROPE 0

Author's Note: Boy Inserted into picture. But you can imagine that can't you?

So, the ultimate question is this: Where does American baseball come from?

One place American baseball comes from is American stickball.

But stop. Imagine going back in time, you as a young American kid, hanging out in the city after school because you have no iPhone, TV, radio, or no amazing Foo Fighters concert to attend. Maybe there is a traveling circus in town, but let's say you can't afford it. You still say, "Hey, Charlie, I really can't play baseball with you today because, well, three hundred years from now, this sport's going to be big. And I want them to know we created it right here. (Suddenly, there is a long, silent pause.) OK. I'll forget writing about it for the history books. Yeah, I'll do it tomorrow. I'm coming."

Here's the point: Teenagers. Young adults. They don't care about history; they never have. They probably never will. They are not going to go look up how rounders was played in England or London—or read about someone's opinion on how people brought some game across the Atlantic. They rarely listen to adults today. Why would they listen to them back then about some game that didn't actually exist? No different.

First, when I say stickball, it is a generic term (perhaps one of a couple names used, like *base ball*) for anything played with a bat and ball in the US before 1846, but urban—driven by the city. So, when historians touch upon the history of baseball, they hardly touch what we could call stickball. The problem is that stickball wasn't always called stickball. It's not like somebody back in history said, "Let's invent a game, and you and I are going to call it stickball. "

But it's usually just *let's play some ball*, right? They called it *ball*. Just some simple name. They weren't thinking that "this is going to be a great sport someday, so we gotta pick a name that is going to last" (the generic term base ball, space in between, was also around).

The second problem here is the fact that stickball wasn't significant enough to be written about. Just because it was not written about doesn't mean it didn't exist. Documentation within a sport that had minimal documentation available only goes so far. Unfortunately, that is the truth.

So, apparently, there are a couple of mentions of stickball and games like that here and there, but the mentions are typically in the context of throwaway lines. Something like this: "You probably had some game, like a bat and ball game, in the US played three hundred years before the beginning of professional, organized baseball."

In his book *Base-ball: How to Become a Player,* published in 1888, New York Base-Ball Club member John Montgomery Ward mentions that he believes our baseball came from youths. He scoffs at rounders and the idea that American *base-ball* is from Europe. In my opinion, without mentioning him by name, he praises as well as takes a swipe at Henry Chadwick for promoting the rounders theory, writing, "...he has lost no opportunity to advance his pet theory."

City youths as major contributors to baseball's origin makes sense based on the nature of sport. You have to prove that that is incorrect; not the other way around. Stickball wasn't so important that it was front page news anywhere. Of course. So that doesn't make it any less real. It's just in the nature of it—you are not going to write a full-page story or have a sports section on *tag*. You're just not going to do it. You are not going to document *stickball*. It's just not going to happen, folks. To say or suggest that stickball wasn't played is to suggest that kids weren't kids. It doesn't make any sense.

Another kind of interesting thing is that a lot of this forms around some big cities. Cities such as New York. A bit of Boston. St Louis. Philly. What's interesting is that the nature and the essence of the sport is coming from clubs too, and they were coming from these cities. And all of that was coming from the spirit of America: competition. New York City. Building a competitive city. We're doing all this stuff. We are building all this stuff. We are creating new stuff. We need a break from it. We like to organize things.

New York is significant, for me anyways, because there is a sense of organization there in that city. And that competitive American spirit, the kind at the core of the American culture, was being brought to this game—that they all knew about. A game that was played on the streets.

You see all those guys who created the Knickerbocker Rules—which are considered perhaps the most important in terms of codifying the sport. (By the way, there is also the Gotham Club, which was nine years before the Knickerbocker Base Ball Club.) For a few of those guys, the game was new. But most of them had seen, even played, the street game somewhere and had extracted the best of the rules from it and made up new rules that made sense.

These were smart guys. These were guys coming from New York City and there is a spirit of competition there that was growing in a city that was growing and increasingly competitive.

Team and club formations accelerated the improvements. You wanna beat that team? I want a better bat—a longer bat to hit it harder. A better ball—harder ball to hit it farther. Better rules. More competitive rules.

A growing entrepreneurial business mentality accelerated it all as well. There is a memoir about a teenager who was creating leather balls for British officers who were prisoners all the way back in 1782, making twenty-five cents per ball. That's kind of cool. But for the record, what he describes were not baseballs, which were still fifty or sixty years away.

Now, what that memoir shows is not that people were writing about British prisoners or about them playing some nonspecific ball game—neither rounders nor townball are mentioned. But what it shows is much more about the American spirit of entrepreneurship—what Spalding, Rawlings, and all these players-turned-entrepreneurs would be doing a hundred years later in the US. What it was showing was proof that the US was fueling an entrepreneurial drive. Even back then, the underlying spirit that would drive and elevate it all was already there.

Here's what American stickball brings to the table that none—none!—of those earlier versions of bat-and-ball games brought: an elevated American attitude. Grit. Fight. And win.

Attitude. Sports. The kind of professional sports that people were going to pay to come see. That happens here in the US. None of those other animals were headed to be the Kentucky Derby horse. The American version was.

So rounders was never headed that way. Cricket did head that way, but it was a completely different sport. And English base-ball, hyphen in between, didn't go that way. German ball didn't. I think part of English base-ball was a professional *tag* game, by the way. I mentioned that because it states it in the rules!

Here is one of those amazing, very subtle hints of what was going on—of the mindset of those times. That American attitude. If you read William Wheaton's interview, you get the gist of it. As mentioned, cricket was not enough exercise for them. And that is what I mean by the American spirit. Let's maximize every element of this sport.

We are all about competition here. I think that is the major difference. And it was found on the streets: "I'm going to kick your butt this afternoon. See you soon!" That attitude is more important than a "footnote" or some document that mentions a word that doesn't even mean *base* as we know it today.

Baseball is not about the physical things. It actually is not. It's not even about the rules. It is not. It's about competition, athleticism, and attitude—the desire and the drive to win: "Let's go play ball and let me kick your butt." That's why it is so much an American sport.

Even Documentation can Serve as Proof

I have found that few researchers write seriously about stickball. Maybe, that is just the way I interpret the silence as well. When you look it up briefly, some articles point to *stickball* as a street game picked up after official baseball began. The opposite is true.

It is a problem if there is an over reliance on documentation when documentation is limited and you are writing about "tag." I say tag again, because it is like stickball. It is a clear example of this: No one was going to write about tag. No one was going to write about stickball. I know I wrote about that, but here is the deeper point:

As mentioned, there is an ordinance found by John Thorn that proves bat-and-ball games were already here in 1791. I will get to that specific ordinance shortly. But what does it really mean? Bat-and-ball games, several of them, were already here in the United States. And that, in part, is what I mean by stickball.

There was also a specific, more competitive version of *stickball* that was emerging within the cities. Think about urban stickball, meaning ball played in the streets of emerging big cities like New York City. The stuff no one was going to document. But the stuff teenagers and young adults craved and loved. It fit them. It fit the city. It fit an emerging America.

Here is a way to think about it in contrast to townball, which first emerged as a community game, not a street game. Think "town festival"—the fifty-players-in-the-outfield version. That led to, as mentioned, the follow-up, let's-do-that-regularly version; these verions were more organized but bascially fueled by fun and not passionate competition. Also, what does that mean? No street employed. They played in parks or designated fields, with a box-shaped layout. No diamond. And, again, no hard ball, no hard pitching, and no baseball *bases*—they used sticks in the ground. You couldn't put a stick into the ground on a street, paved or not, right? That is three-plus strikes against townball right there. Townball would die off.

Meanwhile, a separate activity, stickball, was happening on nearby streets; city street ball was alive. We are talking about a different ball game played within the urban life of big US cities. Harder. A bit faster. Developing at a time when limited transportation limited the world of teenagers and young adults to confined, cemented (or not) neighborhoods without parks close enough by, meaning that they were playing in streets relatively close to their front doors.

Players from the same general city block or urban area played one another. Perhaps parents and other adults wanted kids close enough to home to keep an eye on them. In her acclaimed 1961 book, *The Death and Life of Great American Cities*[36], author Jane Jacobs suggests that what made some urban life safer was all-eyes-on kids; "all-eyes-on" was how she phrased it. Grocers. Tradesmen. Bakers. Barbers. The presence of local merchants served as a unified neighborhood kids watch. Jacobs suggests that children were never far from eyes of the city, which at times—not always—kept many of them out of trouble. In country life that was not possible—and that difference is something most people never thought about before Jane.

So the stickball playing ground was sometimes right outside the front door or just up the block. Pickup games. Broom handles. Makeshift bases. And the geometry of row housing streets and city cross streets were influencing the layout of the bases.

Now, you can go with what I just wrote or not. In any and every case, that still leaves the biggest influence: stickball's DNA. The core. The real deal that made it one of the foundations of baseball.

Something to Cry to Your Mommy About

Stickball is about attitude. That's why American teenagers, actually young adults within an urban environment, loved it. That attitude would fuel changes in the game partly built off of stickball.

Future players and club creators like Wheaton were seeing these games played in the streets. They saw and felt it. What were they learning that was different? Attitude. These street ball players were not about the *community*. They were not about a relaxed time or a Sunday in the park with family and friends. They were about "sending you home crying to your mommy" or "don't worry; tomorrow, I am going get my revenge and kick your butt. See ya then, sucka."

Others who played stickball or street ball were young adult workers who worked hard and played hard. With limited time, they played in the streets below where they rented rooms. They had all come to the big city in hopes of working there, where the jobs were. Some of them lived right above the grocery or merchandise stores. Perhaps their time was limited, but their need for some type of outlet was not.

Down on these streets or not far away were pickup games that became regular, I'll-get-ya-back competitive rematches. It was a way to blow off steam after a hard day's work. They didn't have time and didn't want to travel too far. They just had one another, a ball, and a stick or broom of some kind. But most importantly, they had attitude.

I wrote that a real strike was about "sending you home crying to your mommy" and "strike-your-butt-out" a few times. Those lines capture the essence of the truth in a visceral, urban-city-like way because they reflect the real attitude inherent in US stickball brought to what would be this club-driven new game categorized under the generic term *base ball* and soon to be called *baseball* as the name of a specific sport.

Think about rock and roll music—the high energy that connected it to youth. Suggested by its own name, townball was more like classical music not rock and roll. (Now, I love classical music but not for higher-energy, rock and roll dancing, right?). It was probably a matter of degree, but townball was not really driven by or founded on this charged, somewhat rock and roll-like, one-on-one, competitive, athletic-driven attitude found in big city urban streets. No one wants to cry at a community festival unless you're a kid who just dropped his ice cream. By the way, in the early 1800s, ice cream was considered exotic—more reason to cry.

With adult sports enthusiasts, young professionals, there was a new attitude found here in the city. Indeed, it was coupled with a love of exercise and athleticism: It is the reason cricket doesn't make the cut in the United States either. Wheaton addresses it directly in his interview, saying this:

> **Myself and intimates, young merchants, lawyers, and physicians found cricket too slow and lazy a game. Three-cornered cat was a boy's game, and did well enough for slight youngsters but it was a dangerous game for powerful men.**[37]

Wheaton is talking about a young adult game grounded in real athleticism, professionalism, and competition. He was also describing a new approach, a new attitude, that was not found in these other games. Those others lacked true baseball DNA, if you will, so a new game was constructed. There again is another proof. Because this new baseball had the right DNA, the new game exploded in interest. Bye-bye townball. Forever.

What you are reading about throughout this book is layers upon layers of deeper and deeper concepts that move us from the superficial—stick and ball or even bat-and-ball—to the core essence of the sport that makes it baseball—what it is today. The perfect sport.

Why All the Pretenders Strike Out

For every reason historians give that rounders, townball, and all of these other pretenders are like American baseball, superficially, there are ten reasons they are not. The essence of baseball is not there. Reasoning based on the superficial—like some game's use of a bat and ball—just sounds good.

American baseball has the legends, the heroes, the reporters, the signed autographs, the leagues, and the club teams. So why did I mention that? It's the difference between a sport and a game. Rounders and townball are games. They're not sports.

Imagine if we used the overhand throw found in the Massachusetts Game (Town Ball) rules in a World Series today: "The Ball must be thrown—not pitched or tossed—to the Bat, on the side preferred by the Striker, and within reach of his Bat." (the Massachusetts Game rules, May 13, 1858).

Within reach of his bat? On the side *preferred* by the Striker? In other words, in his sweet spot (just thrown, with no intention to strike the player out.)

SMACK! Over the fence. Bye-bye!

CHAPTER TWENTY

1884:
THE BIGGEST
PITCH OF ALL

American Baseball Comes from American Baseball

So, there is a twist in the statement above: If you notice, I am not saying from America. The twist is I am saying American baseball itself. That is something that isn't obvious until it is.

It is the grand twist. It is an unexpected historical twist in this whole game, if you will, of proving that baseball comes from the United States and not Europe. What the concept modeling allowed me to see, in a eureka moment, was that baseball, American baseball, actually comes from itself. And if that is true—and it is—then Europe can no longer be considered the origin of baseball.

A Shift In Emphasis, Means a Shift In Its Nature, Shown in Results

In 1846—in the first official game—they were pitching underhand. In 1883, they decided to allow sidearm pitching in American baseball. The next year they allowed overhand pitching for the first time officially—that is when the game changed. The essence of baseball finds its core in pitching and, by extension, batting. It is so obvious. But it's also so important. The key in history is that everything relates to that.

So what is 1884 and this period from 1846 to 1884 telling us?

At the core of it, the distinguishing feature, and there are many, but the primary distinguishing feature that changes and revolutionizes the game or completes it—what we know as baseball today—is the overhand pitch. And that doesn't happen till thirty-eight years into the sport we call "American baseball."

In other words, the very first game in 1846 (some say 1845) was technically the beginning of the organizational aspect of American baseball. But it still lacked a core concept found at the heart (or essence) of baseball: The I-am-going-to-strike-your-butt-out pitching. (The kind of attitude naturally found in street or stickball.) It wasn't until 1884—when overhand pitching was officially allowed in the sport—that true baseball came to be. Abbott meets Costello. John, Paul and George meet Ringo. H_2 meets O. Whatever analogy you want to use. The year 1884 was when baseball put it all together and became the game we know today. The perfect sport.

We move from something that's going toward baseball—which American baseball was—to something that *is* American baseball.

Everything in that sport begins with pitching, and I mean overhand pitching—fastballs, sliders, and so on—and with catching all the statistics that are generated from the pitcher and batter duel.

If there isn't overhand pitching, it's not baseball.

So if you're even stepping into anything that happened in any other country before 1846, you will not find overhand, professional-level pitching. And that is the essence of the sport. When we have the overhand pitch, suddenly the sport is actually all there.

Real pitching must involve the intention of striking the batter out. Thank you, Jim Creighton. That leads to pitchers innovating ways to strike you out. Thank you, Candy Cummings, who introduced the first curveball in 1867. Why? Because pitchers were looking to strike batters out, not just serve them opportunities. In 1883, they officially allowed side-arm pitching in the game.

Finally, in 1884, it all comes to full force with overhand pitching.

So none of these sports from Europe had the strike-your-butt-out pitching concept (that stickball attitude), though you can imagine some rival players approached that line. But in previous times that would have been against the rules and certainly less safe.

So My Biggest Pitch of All Is the Significance of the Year 1884

Let me start with a reminder based on the critical relationship between pitching and real American baseball. Let me use an analogy to lock this down:

Humankind didn't fly, couldn't fly, and wasn't flying till people got aerodynamics right. Baseball didn't exist, couldn't exist, and wasn't baseball in its essence till they got pitching right.

It is also the ultimate proof baseball comes from the United States. This fact also has a major implication. Now, I know and understand that this may not be what some want to hear. Yet it is also great news because it is critically important to proving what we do want to hear.

If true, and it is, that means that the year 1884 is the true beginning of American baseball. That's when the essence of the sport is all there. That is why Europe is not the source of American baseball.

When we apply concept modeling to baseball, here is what we find. A baseball is not about any kind of ball, but a leather *hardball* with stitching that allows for hard fastballs and curveballs. A stick, or even a well-crafted stick, is not a *crafted weapon of choice*—a bat meant to fight a duel against a pitcher intending to get the batter out. A *base* is not a pedestal, or a stone, or a boulder, or a brickbat, or a stick in the ground. A baseball base is based on the sand bags, or bags-filled-with-sand idea. And *base* as a concept goes deeper. That means a foot-oriented, stat-plat where distance/placement is important and where a bag is far safer when used in competitive play that was driven by an emerging, competitive, athletic-loving United States. A *glove-free* hand is not the same as a *hand-with-a-glove* that features a pocket or web—something that *augments* a player's catching abilities for an elevated competition.

From a concept modeling point of view, the core essence of baseball is all here in 1884. Baseball has arrived. It is not about "coming soon to a park near you." Real baseball is here, homegrown in the USA—stamped down forever in 1884.

The Kentucky Derby is not about cow racing. It's about horse racing. That is why Europe is not the source of American baseball.

CHAPTER TWENTY-ONE

FOUR FOUL BALLS

As you know, Occam's razor is the problem-solving theory or principle that suggests that the simpler explanations are more likely to be correct. Here, we briefly want to mention four simple issues.

Foul Ball One: Bat-and-Ball as a Category or Even Ball as a Category

This is a subtle shift in understanding concept. The category of bat-and-ball is exclusionary, not inclusionary. If you make that concept mistake, it's a big problem.

What do I mean by *exclusionary* as a concept, not just a word? It's meant to keep other games, other things, out. It's not really telling you anything about something inside the category. Anything inside that category is not automatically related to something else inside that category. It just isn't. Even though you think it's related, it's not.

Let me give you an example: Let's say we had a category called water sports. That's to exclude land sports and perhaps a few air sports if you want to get technical. But it doesn't mean that water polo is related to surfing. Right? They're both included in that category but they're not related at all. Otherwise you might be able to say that surfing is the source of water polo.

Let me show you some reasons why you could say that: They both involve water. OK. They both involve people getting wet. OK. They both involve people swimming. They both require that you wear a bathing suit, probably. So we could continue. They are both athletic sports. They both require the use of your arms to paddle. If you wanted to, you could create a list of how they're related, but they are not related.

Bat and ball are just two of the most basic things on the planet, especially when you consider a bat is actually a stick. And then you are going back to prehistory with that, folks.

So that category, bat-and-ball, doesn't tell us anything. And you have to be very, very careful—because it naturally pushes people into the assumption that anything that came before any other bat-and-ball sport is the origin of the latter bat-and-ball sport. And that is the argument that happens when people unofficially but widely use a category called *bat-and-ball*. Like the category of water, it is just too broad. So the category itself is probably what leads to some of the issues here.

Foul Ball Two: Looking for Baseball in Children's Games

There's a theory that baseball comes from the Tudor dynasty because shortly thereafter and during that period the words like *ball or stoole ball* seems to appear.

As mentioned, In the year 1744, a book is published, and it's an amazing book. We've already mentioned it a couple of times. It is called *A Little Pretty Pocket-Book*, by John Newberry.

Newberry, as I wrote, became famous for writing kids' books. First of all, researchers say it is the first book to use the actual word "base-ball." So here's where one of the notions that baseball was invented by the Tudor dynasty comes from.

The Occam-simple point is that we're looking for baseball in children's books. That does not work. Now, it may seem like a contradiction that I devoted a chapter to tag and the like, yet here I am suggesting that looking for baseball in a children's game is a mistake. But it is not—especially when you consider the *essence* of a thing. Even if elements can look similar, the concept of *amusement* is completely different from the concept of *professional sports competition*. Both a surgeon and a killer can cut into a man's flesh, but the essence of those two acts are very different.

After that, do I have to say it? Baseball, American baseball, does not come from a book dedicated to children's amusements. It wasn't the same sport. Young adults, perhaps older teenagers, drove the creation of the game of baseball in the United States, not children. Folks, you need the competitive grit found in baseball.

At the other end of the scale, baseball coming from Europe is not proven by the word *base ball* as mentioned in a great author's novel either. In other words, baseball doesn't come from Europe just because Jane Austen wrote a novel in which a word—not our word—*base ball* was mentioned. The simple issue is that Jane's use of the word base ball doesn't mean "baseball." As mentioned, in those days, the word baseball could be better interpreted as "pedestal ball" or just ball.

For the record, the book that Jane Austin wrote that mentions *base ball* was called Northanger Abbey—completed about 1798 and later published in 1817. For those who are interested, the appendix of this book offers a segment presented as a scene (a script) on what would happen if all the theories around baseball's origin from the 1700s were set within a fictional, competitive-level, professional-baseball game, only this one offers us Jane Austin as a color commentator. I use the budding romantic relationship found in *Pride and Prejudice*, perhaps Jane's greatest novel, to inspire the interaction of the broadcast announcers calling our fictional baseball game at a fictional **Tudor Memorial Stadium**. Did I strike out with that piece? You be the ump.

Foul Ball Three: Overlooking Stats and Scoring Changes?

Rounders, English base-ball, German ball, Scandinavian longball, France's poison ball, tut-ball, stoolball, cats—there were all these games and more before 1828, but none of them had stats.

As stated, American baseball was, is, and will always be about stats. In baseball, stats are not an afterthought. It's in the DNA. As you probably know from anthropology, there have been a lot of humanoids—like Neanderthal man—but as it turns out, they didn't become us. It has to be in the DNA, and it wasn't.

But there is something else we need to cover:

Amazingly, baseball here in the United States is the only sport that I know of that actually put in rules that reduced scoring. For a sport driving explosive fan-growth, that must have been seen as a big risk. To my knowledge, no other sport has done that; most have actually added to scoring. Football added the extra point and the two-point play. I would throw a safety in there as well. Basketball added the highly successful three-point play. Soccer? Well, it stayed rather consistent—a goal is always one point. But it did add the penalty kick rule in 1890 (the first actual penalty kick inside a game happened in 1891). Later, it would add stricter rules to protect strikers, or frontline scorers, and demonstratively increase scoring.

In the United States, the introduction and nature of strikes and real pitching reduced scoring. As mentioned, early games were high scoring. Pitching, real pitching, reduced that. You have to consider that doing that might have been controversial at first and might have scared some of those in charge of establishing the rules within baseball. Imagine the impact on some of the fans. One might think that instead of having a game producing twenty-plus (even forty-plus) runs scored, a game where there are only two, or say three, would kill attendance. That may be why the change from underhand to official overhand took basically thirty-eight years.

My hunch is that slowly, the competitive nature of the sport took hold. Slowly, fans and official rule-makers alike saw that real pitching made the sport more competitive. Exciting. It elevated it into something powerful and new, and it ultimately perfected the sport.

It now meant something special to get a hit. And a hit became a real stat; it meant something significant. The distance to first base meant something. The layout of the field meant something. The

count, meaning the number of foul balls to strikes built some anticipation. Excitement. The concept of *stats* that was inherent in the game would soon be used to grow the game exponentially.

There is no doubt that the introduction of the box score by Henry Chadwick helped influence the change. Readers could see the change in black and white. At first, pitchers were becoming stars—they were hard to hit off of. But batters began to fight back, and with both the introduction of a real baseball bat and the allowance of overhand pitching in 1884, both the essence and the competitive nature of the game were elevated. "Take me out to the ball game! I want to see them bat and battle it out."

The changes also elevated the importance of stats. Other sports do produce stats, but it's really like an afterthought. In baseball, it is *stats* (as a concept) that actually produce the sport. That is the amazing twist. And we can see that in our concept model.

Foul Ball Four: It's Not Called *American Baseball*; Yet It Is Called *America's Game*

It's American baseball and it is obviously so. Not English. Not German. Not French. American baseball. But it's not officially called *American Baseball*, and that is significant. For example, had the sport been based on English Base ball—or any game from England—we would have officially called it *American Baseball* to distinguish it. But it wasn't.

No, the term American baseball is just for emphasis. But because of the amazing way language works, the term *America's Game* actually implies something totally different—that there was a deep-rooted synergy between what was happening in the country at that time and what was developing inside this game inspired in part by Urban streets.

The American spirit, which was infused inside stickball and these American bat-and-ball games, would be leading us toward that national sport. Truly America's game.

America was a place we had to build ourselves. Remember, Rome was already built. And that attitude, that competitive attitude, was found in the creation of a sport that would turn into a business. It's that concept of athleticism—of getting better and better at something. And that's what is found within the essence of a professional sport.

And that was developed here on the streets of the cities. And here in the countryside. And the cities took it to the next level in terms of giving it some organizational structure. And at the end of the day, it became more and more like an organized business.

And that very last point? Yes, it goes back to Abbott and Costello. The ultimate essence of baseball is also found in what Abbott and Costello demonstrate for us, which is *fun!* Entertainment.

You feel that when you listen to Abbott and Costello. You feel it when you watch a good game. Why? Because they are both fun. It is self-evident. Abbott and Costello were professionals. They were working hard to perfect their craft. It was similar to watching a good baseball game. The teams, the managers, the athletes who were playing baseball were also working hard to perfect their craft. That is why it started to head toward a professional, money-making sport.

You begin the creation of professional athletes as baseball players. That's Jim Creighton. Candy Cummings. That's Ty Cobb. Later, Satchel Paige. Guys who worked at getting better at the sport—in other words, their athleticism or athletic ability was honed. The level of their professionalism and their athletic skill made it fun to watch. If you are reading this book, perhaps it is because you in fact find baseball, baseball history, and following the teams, following players, and watching games—all of it—kind of *fun*.

I am sure these European games were fun, but not like American baseball. It was as elevated as they could make it. Later it would translate into stadiums, and even Ball Park Franks. Let me give you a little side note: A saleswoman, Mary Ann Kurk, won a contest in 1958 for coming up with that name inside the company Hygrade Food Products, which made the secret-recipe hot dogs for the Detroit Tigers.

By the way, why I mention that is because trivia also makes baseball fun. How fun is trivia? Very.

CHAPTER TWENTY-TWO

GRAPHIC PROOF

Graphically Speaking, *Conceptually Speaking*, European Games Just Didn't Cut It

Just for fun, which is also in the nature of baseball, I decided to put most of the concept models together to see what that might tell us about where baseball came from. For the record, some of these models could still be developed further. Concept models are like a soup: You can let them simmer a bit and go back later and taste-test them. In other words, you can step away, come back later, and find some new insight that you did not see. Something deeper.

In very graphic terms, no early European contender holds all the concepts found in American baseball. It is not even close. Why? Because almost everything you see within the combined graphics came from the United States. Not Europe.

Think of this as the ultimate fossil; use it as such. As an anthropologist might, measure any other game ever invented in Europe or before to see where it stands in relationship to our American baseball. They all strike out.

Combined Baseball Concept Model

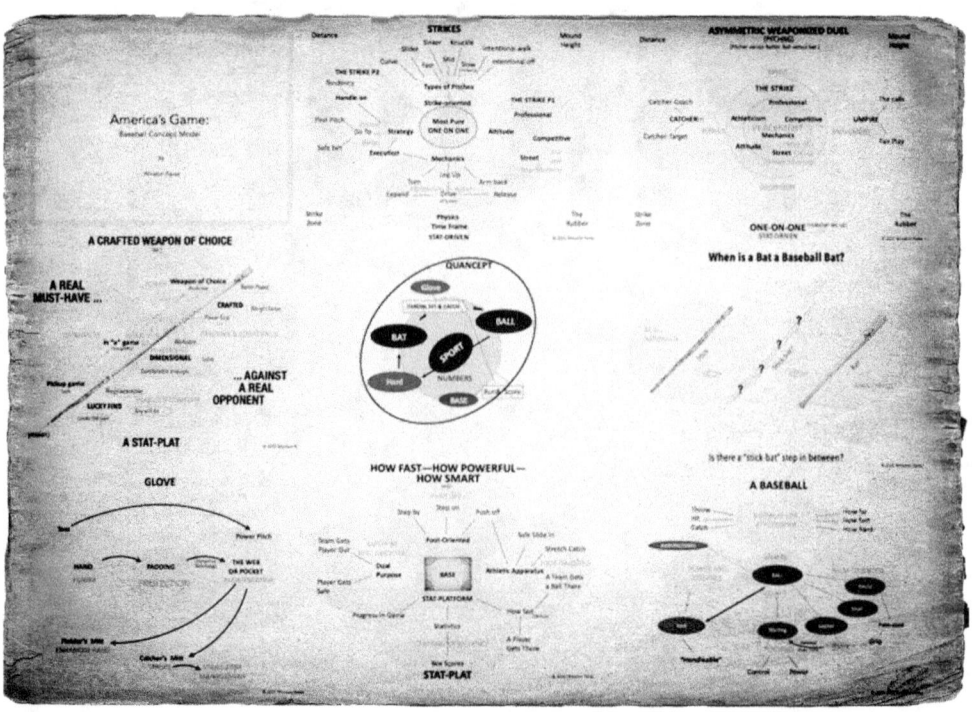

Fig. 30: Combined Baseball Concept Model by Winston J Perez Copyright 2022 Winston J Perez

As graphically illustrated above, the sheer number of concepts related to American baseball that cannot be found in these games coming from Europe represents nail in the coffins for rounders, townball, and all the other pretenders.

For every reason people give that rounders, townball, and all of these other pretenders are like American baseball, superficially, there are ten times ten reasons they are not.

Concept tends toward the infinite in nature. That just means that there is a ton of more information locked away in the essence of something than what you might see superficially.

CHAPTER TWENTY-THREE
SOUND PROOF

So where does this all go?

This goes straight to my favorite proof baseball comes from the United States. That proof is found not in a physical thing, or a document, but something even more powerful. And absolutely everyone who has ever seen baseball at a ballpark knows it: the Fantastic Fan Favorite Sound.

It also goes back to concept modeling. The baseball concept model helped me see an obvious truth, one stemming from the physical nature of baseball, meaning the use of real baseballs, real baseball bats, and real pitching as they were developed here in the United States. Not Europe.

So let me get to what I call the Fantastic Fan Favorite Sound which, when used as evidence, is literally "sound proof." It is a proof that baseball originated in the United States and that proof is very—well—sound.

The creation and evolution of baseball's distinct tools, apparatuses, and equipment meant that the world was being introduced to a new sound. It was a sound not found in any of the contenders or pretenders from Europe. How about cricket? With its flat-faced bat, it does come close; for real fans, it is not close enough. (Cricket is a great, but different, sport.)

And everyone reading this knows that distinctive sound; it is only made possible by three things: an American baseball, an American ball, and an American baseball pitcher's powerful, overhand pitch. That sound is the—*crack!*—of a home run hit. And it is, as Babe Ruth would prove, the sound that literally and figuratively fills stadiums to capacity.

It's the difference between, on the one hand, a cudgel as they sometimes called it, (a much shorter hitting apparatus) that strikes a much softer ball so that it travels to an outfield and, on the other hand, a Louisville Slugger wielded by a professional batter who powers a hit over the Fenway Park Green Monster. The power, the sound, the beauty of that is felt by over 35,000 people in a sold-out stadium.

For the record, even if cricket came close, our home run—*crack!*—sound is unique. It helped take the growing interest in baseball to a new, explosive level.

I am not a sound engineer, but I believe that sound was officially introduced and brought to full, crowd-winning, stadium-rocking perfection when it was brought inside the first US baseball stadium—inside the echoing walls of Ebbets Field in Brooklyn on April 5, 1913. That sound would have been heard by a sold-out crowd of 30,000 inside the stadium and perhaps still another 5,000 fans standing around outside the stadium. The sound would have been followed by the very first full stadium crowd *roar!* Oh, man. That two-part explosion must have been thrilling. Below is from the New York Times, April 6, 1913:

Brooklyn outfielder Casey Stengel stole the show in the first game ever played in Ebbets Field on April 5, 1913. . . . Stengel hit the park's first home run in a 3-2 exhibition win over the New York Yankees.[38]

In less than four one-hundredths of a second, America was introduced to an awesome new sound—an inside a packed stadium home run slam. The full measure of it.

That sound was not found in rounders. That sound was not found in townball. It was not found in stoolball, tut-ball or English base ball. It was not found in German ball, långboll, or poison ball. It was unique to this American game that had its own name: baseball. Going, going, —*SMACK*—gone!

CHAPTER TWENTY-FOUR

BATBALL? OH YEAH! PROOF!

Email me at info@conceptmodeling.com, and tell me if what I write next seems true. I'd be curious.

I don't know if you ever thought of this. And yet it is so obvious when you hear the sound of a **ball** hit by a **bat**. *Wham!* What would you be hearing in that moment? You would literally be hearing something at the very core of the sport: You would be hearing the word—or concept of—"batball" in action. This is how its abstract essence translates into the material world. And amazingly, you are not hearing *base*, like a player sliding into second base—as in the word **base**ball

Batball. A core concept found at the heart of the sport. By the way, because of evolution of the bat, you would also be hearing "stickball." It's the essence-based origin of the word; something grafted into shape for a specific action, reason, or even *mission*. A "bat" used for playing a specific sport. (For those of you keeping stats, I am not saying we should call the sport either *stickball* or *batball*.)

In following the concept model, basically our fossil, I was using *batball* to find baseball's true origin. I didn't know how, where, or even if it would show up. But the concept model suggested it would be out there, somewhere, and maybe insightful or even important.

Then all of a sudden, a home run came my way. John Thorn points it out in an article and in his great book *Baseball in the Garden of Eden*. His book points out a 1791 city ordinance prohibiting bat and ball games near or around their meeting house. That implies that there were a lot of people already playing a game called *base ball* or even baseball. (You have to account for loose spelling at that time.)

Thank You, John Thorn: The Personal Conclusion to My Story

And yes. Suddenly, there it was: the word "batball"—what Thorn called a "conundrum." Some were asking, "What is batball?" What is batball? It is proof.

Why? Because we go back to our concept model from part I. Those two most obvious questions that we started with and the fact that our concept model dictated that you have to look for "batball" to find American baseball.

And that was solid gold to me. That is huge because it says several things: First, bat-and-ball games, and I include stickball, were here before *The Boy's Own Book* and they were here thirty-seven years before the first mention of rounders in that 1828 book.

It is also proof about *stickball*. When you look up stickball online now, it states that it came after major league baseball. But the truth, confirmed by that document in 1791, is that stickball, again as a generic (street-oriented) term, likely existed before major league baseball. It is generic because nobody was going to officially call a sport "stickball." Did youth play a bat-and-ball game in the streets in 1791? Near a said city *meeting house*? Of course. It is the reason for the city ordinance.

Keep in mind, like the rules themselves, names and generic terms for these games were being naturally worked out as well. *Base ball* (as opposed to *baseball* as one word) would clearly become a generic term. *The Base Ball Player's Pocket Companion* published almost 70 years later (1859) suggests that it did serve as that for a time. Stickball is also a generic term (what I would use to distinguish more gritty games) perhaps geared to an urban setting, but also used for more specific city street-based games, as the gritty name suggests—stick!

If researchers are using just the word "base-ball"—one word—found in a 1744 children's book, when it doesn't even mean baseball as we know it, then they should consider the 1791 city ordinance as proof that a collection of bat-and-ball games or ball games existed here thirty-seven years before that 1828 book mentions rounders. The ordinance mentions games that had obviously been well-known before 1791.

I wrote that the great MLB historian John Thorn found that critical document—from 1791. Here is that Pittsfield, Massachusetts, ordinance.

No Person or Inhabitant of said town, shall be permitted to play any game of wicket, cricket, baseball, batball, football, cats, fives, or any other game played with a ball within the distance of eighty yards from said meeting house.[39][40]

First, it is so specific, and yet there is **no mention of townball**, strongly suggesting it was not the source of American baseball. That is telling. **No mention of rounders either.** So going back to Ken Burns' *Baseball* documentary for a second. Here is what it says at twenty-two minutes and thirty-three second in:

By the 1800s, townball and its many variations were played nearly everywhere.

I had to include that *Baseball* quote, not because it is from the highly and rightfully praised documentary film, but because in the end it shows the bad influence that townball theory, and by extension rounders, had through "false advertising," an influence that even extended to the monumental work of Ken Burns' *Baseball*.

The lack of townball being mentioned in the ordinance suggests that townball was not everywhere. Also, it proves that these games were not variations of townball. Remember, the documentation on anything to do with any bat-and-ball game before the 1800s is extraordinarily limited. Townball was just more visible because it was "related" to towns, originally tying it to story-worthy community events and festivities.

But again, what game was one of the games mentioned? **Batball**.

There it is—I had found what I was looking for and what concept modeling on baseball suggested to me: *batball*. It was important to me personally because it was proof that I had done my concept model on baseball correctly.

But finding batball is very important historically because it corrects the direction of the baseball-origin ship. Here is what I mean. Batball, as found in the Pittsfield, Massachusetts, 1791 city ordinance proves that a bat-and-ball game, which cannot be linked to Europe, existed in the USA. You could make that case, directly or indirectly, for the other games listed in the ordinance, but you cannot make that case for *batball*.

It also is clear that there is no proof that townball influenced this game called batball—perhaps the only game right now that cannot be linked in some way to Europe. More importantly, batball cannot be linked to rounders since this ordinance was declared 37 years before the first mention of rounders in *The Boy's Own Book*, 1828.

Am I saying baseball originated from batball. No. Amazingly, the ordinance also mentions the word *baseball*.

That ordinance proves that there were any number of bat-and-ball games, so why did we choose townball as an influence on all the others, when the opposite is probably true.

When that ordinance states "any other game played with a ball," that is to cover things like "ball" or "stickball"—even less formal names for any ball-based game (even the more generic term *base ball*, with space between *base* and *ball*.)

Critically important, it is what I stated before about the nature of bat-and-ball: If every other country has shown spontaneous ability to develop some kind of bat and ball game, why should the USA be any different. Batball proves it is not.

Batball proves that there was a game in the US that cannot be directly or indirectly—not even through word association—linked to Europe. Using the names in the ordinance, we could say that wicket and cricket definitely come from Europe. We could also link both cat and fives to Europe as well. And for the record, we can leave out football. But batball has no provable link to Europe. There is no "batball" game found in Europe—though it is possible that in the future we may find a document that suggest a link, but it is not likely.

Then there is later, forty-six years later. The Gotham Club of New York and even the Knickerbocker Base Ball Club (fifty-five years later) could have called their sport or their clubs by any name. No reason not to, and they probably wanted a name that was a little more "adult," a little more sophisticated, a little more professional. The name *baseball* worked—most likely it was a name generally heard out there in the city or the streets, and that probably was the clincher. It was a name that worked on all fronts.

It also means that *batball* as a name didn't stick even though it was around along with *baseball*. And that is probably why *batball* didn't stick around. The relationship between a *bat* and a *stick* was too close to the street game stickball.

To me it suggests that *stickball* had a major influence on our baseball. If that was not true, they would have simply called the sport what it is: *batball*. Look at it this way; or better still, listen to it this way: *Hardball. Softball. Batball.* When you hear them together, *batball* sounds pretty good. But when you associate *batball* with *stickball*, you probably feel a need to step away from the word *stick* if you are forming a professional club. I strongly suggest that the move away from *stickball* was intentional. And you wouldn't think about that if there was not a strong influence already there. So batball didn't work.

Through this book we have continually deconstructed layer after layer inherent in this thing we call baseball. The truth is that things in the physical world approach the infinite when you talk about the abstract world attached to them—meaning concepts. In simpler words, there are so many puzzle pieces, some of them even moving pieces, that one or two pieces alone don't do justice to the big picture—questions just remain that way. I needed to give readers enough of the puzzle to see the big picture clearly. Would you believe there is still more? There actually is more.

I could wrap up the book right here, but that would do concept modeling, but more importantly baseball, true American baseball, an injustice. We will go even deeper into the very heart of this sport we all love in the final chapter. But shouldn't we first try to tackle the most obvious question of all, first?

What About the Actual Name, "Baseball?"

What about the actual word? The word *baseball* does not come from Europe either. It does not. The reason I say that is because teenagers, young adults, weren't going around looking up history books trying to find it.

Think about it. Don't forget this simple point. If the name had been taken from English Base-ball, they would have called it American Base-ball and they did not do that. That tells you that the name was taken from the US, most likely from the streets—not from Europe. And if it was coming from rounders or townball, they would have called it rounders or townball. But they didn't. They called it baseball, so there is a disconnect there.

Why Were They Calling It Baseball Here?

So there's a much simpler explanation for how they came up with the name "baseball."

But first a personal note: I sort of got hammered by someone because my explanation sounded so simple. But life is simple. You don't need a PhD to come up with the name. You know who came up with the name? Not a PhD.

Teenagers on the street, young adults, came up with the name. How? Well, when they wanted to gather and play the game, there were only a few names they could call it. "Let's play some ball!" That's OK but that's not really a name, is it? So how do you come up with the name "baseball"?

Well, if you're sitting around a group of kids or young adults, and someone pops up and says, "Hey, let's go play. You get the ball, I'll get the bat, and we'll come up with some bases."

So when it comes down to it, there were only three words you could pick. In other words, what is the most concept-based name of the sport you can have? Think of it a little bit like the name of *basketball*. You could call it *dribble-ball*. You could call it *dunk-ball*. But the most basic, simple, name that works for that game, because it has to sound good—that's key—is basketball. The same applies to baseball.

There are only three words you can use. There were no gloves at the time, by the way. So, bat, ball, and base. Let's look at those three words (This is taken from my first book on concept[41]):

Base bat ball
Ball bat base
Bat ball base
Bat… base ball

There it is: Bat . . . **base ball.** *Baseball.* And there you have it. Why was it called baseball? Because it sounds good; that's why. That is an awesome name. It is.

Again, you couldn't say batball because the "bat" is related to the "stick" in stickball, making batball a weaker choice. You can't do that. Could you imagine the World Series of Stickball? No. And again, amazingly, that is a big hint that baseball comes (in part at least) from stickball. It certainly seems that they were consciously stepping away from that street-sounding name. Of course they were!

That's it. This isn't quantum physics. It's a question of what sounds good to youth or young adults. Period. It's simply human nature. The word that is the most concept-based but also sounds good is *baseball*. That is the best name, by far, for the sport. And it is that simple. If you repeat that to someone and they suddenly act indignant because the explanation sounds so simple, just fire back to him or her with this: *Really? This is baseball!*

A Confession to Make

I have a confession to make. You may recall that I wrote, and it is true, that people need the fossil in front of them—I mean a concept model—before doing the research. Without that as a guide, you end up looking for baseball *in* other games—inevitably, *in* the wrong places. Then, I said, you simply have to look for baseball.

But here's what I didn't explain: I didn't explain how you do that. Why? Because the obvious isn't. In other words, it is so obvious that had I told you the secret before, you might have had a tendency to discard it immediately as a twist, a trick, or as a sleight of hand. That is what we all tend to do with the obvious.

But there is one lesson you should remember from history: The twist in the successful creation of the first atom bomb was actually a decision to try the exact opposite, a serious 180-degree change of perspective from an *explosion* to an *implosion*. And it was the *implosion* concept that made the very first Los Alamos bomb work.

So, in our case, with a fossil in hand or a concept model in hand, we can now do the search for baseball the right way. We can do the exact opposite, in a serious 180-degree change of perspective: We don't have to look for baseball *in* rounders. We look for rounders, or any contenders, *in* baseball.

When you start that way, all the mistakes become obvious. Why? Because it leads to the right questions: Where are the stats in rounders? Where is the foot-oriented, American-made base, a bag filled with sand, in townball? Where is the hardball in English base-ball? I could go on.

When you look at it from our concept model point of view, all of a sudden, all the other pretenders collapse.

CHAPTER TWENTY-FIVE

ONE NUMBER ABOVE BASEBALL ANALYTICS

In part I of this book, I talked about one of the core concepts in baseball, which is numbers. And that is true.

But the thing about it is this: Many of you already know that. It is almost obvious now because so many people have brought that discussion to the surface. But realizing how deep it goes is a different matter. Hopefully, part I, part II, and part III of this book, combined, suggest how deep it really goes.

But there is a problem here—because there is something else. You have the material or physical things like the bat, the ball, the glove, the bases, and so on. Then you have the intangible things or abstract things—the things you cannot touch—like base running, pitching, fielding, and batting. But there are even deeper things—like athleticism, competition, winning, and losing. Heroes. Legends. Fans. All the things you cannot physically touch—you cannot actually touch the concept of a hero, you can only touch someone who has been honored with that designation.

But there is one other number, like a point, where all those other numbers—all of the physical things and the abstract things that go into baseball—seem to intersect. That is in the number *one*—and the way it points to one word.

To explain how amazing it truly is, I can use what happened in the 2020 World Series between the LA Dodgers and the Tampa Bay Rays. Both excellent teams.

A personal note: I have not read all the opinions about how this team won or that one lost, but I am willing to bet—and later I will read those opinions to find some supporting insight—they will all point to this number.

It's amazing that the World Series may have come down to one. But first, let me include a series of ones, then a single one.

One man. One decision. One player. One game. Yes, you can include one team too. But most likely, the choice made by the Rays will be speculated-on forever, with no perfect resolution actually.

Ultimately, it may have come down to this: **one moment.**

If you are a baseball fan, you already know that moment. That moment was when the Rays took pitcher Blake Snell out of the game. Replaced him with another pitcher. That was the moment—it came down to when Rays manager Kevin Cash made the decision to replace Blake.

So my reaction to all this is threefold. The first part is my opinion. The second and third are concept based.

Here is my opinion. I think it is rather simple, but painful. I think it was what Cash had to do. But it was the wrong decision.

Cash had to take Snell out, according to the theory that the team was built on and was living on. You could say, and it would be true, that the Rays were going to live and die by the analytics, or, yes, strictly the numbers approach that they had been using to run the team and their season.

The fact is, they lived pretty well. Amazingly well. They shocked the baseball world with their strict and successful adherence to what some say was a ruthless—others say savvy—approach, grounding it all in numbers applied to the team, the season, and the Rays' philosophy.

By the way, and it is fascinating to me, that is exactly—I mean exactly—what Neils Bohr and his team did in the development of quantum physics, or more precisely quantum mechanics (used interchangeably today), which you may know revolutionized the entire world, launching the most successful branch of physics of all time. (I should note that Max Planck is also considered the father of quantum theory. It could be an interesting target for concept modeling. Maybe someday.)

In other words, Tampa Bay stuck to the numbers no matter what. That did two things at that moment: It made Cash's decision very clear. And it left him with no other choice. The team had gotten to the sixth game of the world series using that approach. It had proved it could get you there, to almost the very top, to the penultimate peak of success.

There was absolutely no way the team could turn its back on what got it there. And if Cash had left Blake in the game to continue pitching and he had suddenly failed, that is the question everyone would have had to ask: "You got this far, so why didn't you trust or stick with what got you here? Why?"

From their approach, their philosophy, their plan—their all—it was the right decision. It just happened to be the wrong decision. How can we say that? Well, one fact is clear: the Rays lost. But there is always some leeway in that statement because we will never know.

So my opinion is this: Cash made the right decision; it just happened to be wrong. It is also not the decision I would have made. And that leads me to this: who cares what decision I would have made? But really, it leads to this even deeper concept.

The real question is this: Is everything in life just based on the material, the physical? The physics? The science? The numbers? Related to this book, does baseball just come down to numbers? I am not trying to be flippant here, but the answer is yes and no. Why? Because it all points to another number. Another one: ***one chance at glory.***

Glory doesn't make any sense at all if you look at just numbers. Just physics. Just physical things. Glory is a concept. You see the concept of individual glory—what Blake was seeking for deep down—would suggest that Snell would have risen above the numbers—the analytics alone.

Allow me, indulge me, and let me go as deep as possible using what I remind people who are struggling with this thing or that in their life.

The event that reflects it best for me is Kirk Gibson's winning home run with the Dodgers in the 1988 World Series—game one, October 15, 1988. Vin Scully calling the game. It was the bottom of the ninth, the Dodgers were down by a run, and they had two outs with a man on base, with Kirk Gibson coming up to bat. He limps up to the plate because he's injured.

And sure enough, after successive foul balls, a couple of strikes, and even a step-back away from the plate to regain his focus, he slams—*wham!*—a towering home run. And Vin Scully calling the following glorious moments perfectly. *Perfectly!* Many people also remember an iconic moment: Dodgers manager Tommy Lasorda stepping out of the dugout and bounding up and down in pure joy after the hit. (Tommy, having just passed away on January 7, 2021, will be missed by baseball fans.)

Here is my main point: If you hit a home run, it may not mean anything. It is actually just a home run: a ball hit over a fence. And if you are up by eight and you hit another home run to make it up by nine, and you win by nine, that home run probably means nothing—except to the individual player. For the team, it absolutely means nothing.

We forget that the glory for that moment comes from being down.

From being down in the bottom of the ninth. From being down in the bottom of the ninth with two outs. Let me continue: From being down in the bottom of the ninth with two outs with a player who is injured coming up to bat; and the team is on the precipice of losing.

So, I tell you, my friend, if you want real glory, it often comes on the edge of failure.

If you are depressed, you find it in hanging in there another day. If you are about to lose your business, you're attaining glory by continuing to fight the next day.

Real glory comes from all the numbers in baseball going against you: The bottom of the ninth. Two outs. Down by a run. And you are injured, as we all are in some way. It's the number *one* in baseball, elevated by one concept: the concept of glory. One moment. One person. One hit. One home run.

Yes, baseball has numbers at its core, but as it turns out baseball is not just about numbers. Perhaps overlooked, the deepest concept found in baseball is a thing we call glory—unifying team glory, city and citizens glory, and the ultimate stunning power of individual glory.

The question you have to ask—the question I cannot answer for you—is this: Why should all that, the numbers, lead to glory? Unless this thing called glory is real.

Unless that, ultimately, is the essence of all of it. You know, folks, I leave it at that: We started with the obvious. And we end with the obvious. Why? Because The Obvious Isn't.

THE END ...or better... GAME OVER!

POST GAME ANALYSIS:
If concept modeling can do this for baseball, what could it do for your idea, your business, your script, or your product? Have questions? Find out more. Write to us. Stay in touch. Get into our game, join us on our journey. *The Obvious Isn't . . .* is just getting started. info@conceptmodeling.com

Appendix I

William Wheaton's Game-Changer Interview

"How Baseball Began—A Member of the Gotham Club of Fifty Years Ago Tells About It."

San Francisco Examiner, **November 27, 1887.**

Excerpt: William Wheaton Talks About Early Baseball in the US

"...In fact we all were [fond of physical exercise] in those days, and we sought it wherever it could be found. Myself and intimates, young merchants, lawyers, and physicians found cricket too slow and lazy a game. Three-cornered cat was a boy's game, and did well enough for slight youngsters, but it was a dangerous game for powerful men, because the ball was made of a hard rubber center, tightly wrapped with yarn, and in the hands of a strong-armed man it was a terrible missile, and sometimes had fatal results when it came in contact with a delicate part of the player's anatomy.

"**We had to have a good outdoor game, and as the games then in vogue didn't suit us, we decided to remodel three-cornered cat and make a new game.**

"We first organized what we called the Gotham Baseball Club. This was the first ball organization in the United States, and it was completed in 1837. Among the members were Dr. John Miller, a popular physician of that day; John Murphy, a well-known hotel-keeper, and James Lee, President of the New York Chamber of Commerce.

"**The first step we took in making baseball was to abolish the rule of throwing the ball at the runner and ordered that it should be thrown to the baseman instead, who had to touch the runner with it before he reached the base.** During the regime of three-cornered cat there were no regular bases, but only such permanent objects as a bedded boulder or an old stump, and often the diamond looked strangely like an irregular polygon. We laid out the ground at Madison square [sic] in the form of an accurate diamond, with home-plate and sand bags for bases. You must remember that what is now called Madison square [sic], opposite the Fifth Avenue Hotel, in the thirties was out in the country, far from the city limits.

"We had no short-stop, and often played with only six or seven men on a side. The scorer kept the game in a book we had made for that purpose, and it was he who decided all disputed points. The modern umpire and his tribulations were unknown to us. We played for fun and health, and won every time.

"**The pitcher really pitched the ball and underhand throwing was forbidden. Moreover he pitched the ball so that the batsman could strike it and give some work to fielders.** The men outside the diamond always placed themselves where they could do the most good and take part in the game.

"After the Gotham club had been in existence a few months, it was found necessary to reduce the rules of the new game to writing. This work fell to my hands, and the code I then formulated is substantially that in use today. We abandoned the old rule of putting out on the first bound and confined it to fly catching. The Gothams played a game of ball with the Star Cricket Club of Brooklyn, and beat the Englishmen out of sight, of course. That game and the return were the only matches ever played by the first baseball club.

"**The new game** quickly became very popular with New Yorkers, and the numbers of the club soon swelled beyond the fastidious notions of some of us, and we decided to withdraw and found a new organization, which we called the Knickerbocker. For a playground we chose the Elysian Fields of Hoboken, just across the Hudson River. And those fields were truly Elysian to us in those days. There was a broad firm, greensward, fringed with fine shady trees, where we could recline during intervals, when waiting for a strike, and take a refreshing rest.

"We played no exhibition or match games, but often our families would come over and look on with much enjoyment. Then we used to have dinner in the middle of the day, and twice a week we would spend the whole afternoon in ball play. We were all mature men and in business, but we didn't have too much of it as they do nowadays. There was none of that hurry and worry so characteristic of the present New York. We enjoyed life and didn't wear out so fast. In the old game when a man struck out those of his side who happened to be on the bases had to come in and lose that chance of making a run. We changed that and made the rule which holds good now.

"When I saw the game between the Unions and the Bohemians the other day, I said to myself—If some of my old playmates who have been dead forty years could arise and see this game they would declare it was the same old game we used to play in the Elysian Fields, with the exception of the short-stop, the umpire, and such slight variations as the swift underhand throw, the masked catcher, and the uniforms of the players. We started out to make a game simply for safe and healthy recreation. Now it seems, baseball is play for money, and has become a regular business."

Note: Researcher Randall Brown found the article and determined this interview was indeed given by William Wheaton.

TUDOR FANTASY BASEBALL

Winston J. Perez

Baseball is about fun. So what happens if you put all the origin stories and elements together? Well, the next page begins my version of what that might look like in script form. Somewhat anyways. For the record, "(CON'T)" means continued. Welcome to the year 1744 and the Tudor Dynasty Baseball League.

EXT. TUDOR MEMORIAL STADIUM - JULY 1744

Before the "broadcast" starts, we here this announcer up along the Hampton Castle battlements shouting down to the peasant crowd standing around a kind of baseball field where massive jousting competitions generally took place.

> ANNOUNCER (V.O.)
> Let's go back in time, to the playing field of our imagination again. Here are a couple of game announcers sitting by Tudor Memorial Stadium—also called the Hampton Court Stadium. Welcome to our game, July 4, 1744.

We hear an umpire of sorts: *Strike!* Then we hear,

> DARCY
> We have our booth up here between the battlements looking down on a beautiful playing field. It has been a bright sunny day so far. A perfect summer day for a game of, what do you call it, Leslie?

> LESLIE
> Ball. No sign of the plague this weekend. Great day for some ball!

> DARCY
> Indeed. The Tudor Purple and Gold Sox versus the Northern York Yankshiers. I am Mr. Vince Darcy, your play-by-play man, sitting next to Leslie Bingley, our color commentator.
> Also, we are so proud to have with us today a guest commentator, Jane Austen herself.

> JANE AUSTEN
> I am all astonishment. My idea of good company is the company of clever and well-informed people who have a great deal of conversation. This would do very well.

> LESLIE
> Ah, stats. You must mean game stats. Eh, Miss Austen?

DARCY
Well, we are all delighted. Well, speaking of
which, how do these teams stack up, Leslie?

LESLIE
Yes, yes. Both excellent teams.
Excellent records this year.
The P and G Sox come in with
twenty-seven wins, five losses.
Almost the exact opposite of last year.
While the NY Shiers are close behind
their post-dynasty heals at
twenty-five wins and seven losses.

DARCY
What accounts for the dramatic
turnaround for the Sox?

LESLIE
Excellent trades made the last
couple of years.

DARCY
And what about the star pitching
acquisition? Made any difference?
Have you heard of her, Jane?

JANE AUSTEN
I read somewhere that she is
absolutely the difference.

LESLIE
That acquisition is on the mound now.
Indeed. Your viewers are in for a treat

JANE AUSTEN
A pitcher of some consequence. Elegant.
Well-bred. Catapult power of a delicate arm.

LESLIE
There's no shying away from it now.
Time to show the audience hordes
why this one is paid the big shillings, eh?

JANE AUSTEN
My feelings will not be repressed.
You must allow me to tell your viewers
how ardently I admire and
love that eight-year-old
hundred-mile-an-hour-plus
fastball pitcher.

LESLIE
The golden arm of sports royalty. Pitcher
extraordinaire. Young, there on the mound,
kicking around a little dirt to establish a better
foothold. No rubber. No rubber there.
Have to build it yourself, you do;
knows what to do, that pitcher does.
This is what the fuss is all about:
A pitcher with only one loss this season;
outstanding record the last two seasons
with a 2.6 ERA, 293 strikeouts,
137 complete games, and 40 shutouts.
Count them: 40.

DARCY
That was a 95-mile-an-hour curveball.
What do you think, Jane?

JANE AUSTEN
Emotions and childhood are feelings.
They come and go. But the reality of
this pitcher in this game
may stay with us forever.
She is a woman of note—
of incomparable value.

LESLIE
Excellent form. Excellent form.

DARCY
Pretty Miss Polly comes into this game
with only one loss. Overall, the team is
twenty-five and seven, and it is nine
and one in the last ten games.

JANE AUSTEN
And, yes, show me no prejudice,
Mr. Darcy. You must concede that
an eight-year-old, female,

> JANE AUSTEN (CON'T)
> 95-mile-an-hour spitball pitcher
> is of consequence this year of 1744.

> DARCY
> Of some consequence, yes. I believe
> they are about to dedicate a book to her
> and her brother. Leslie, is that who
> I think it is coming to the plate?

> LESLIE
> Yes indeed—hang on.
> This is where it gets exciting.
> He is four-time MVP.

Jane cuts in.

> JANE AUSTEN
> Most valuable prince is it?

> LESLIE
> Ha ha. A little royal humor there, eh?

> JANE AUSTEN
> They say they're ready to pronounce
> and crown him the king.

> LESLIE
> Ha ha. But I would! Coming here with
> a .406 batting average, 30 stolen bases,
> 45 home runs, and a 135-shillings-per-year
> endorsement contract from
> Kill All Huns breakfast cereal.

> JANE AUSTEN
> All of ten years old. Darling. Lord
> Master Tommy. So very proud looking.
> Standing there at home plate.

> LESLIE
> Lord Master Tommy he is—at the ready.

> DARCY
> Looking into the royal box seats, I see
> the commissioner of the league is here—
> King George himself. Is that Vicar Collins
> next to him?

Showing immediate hostility as she eyes the Vicar, Jane chimes in:

> JANE AUSTEN
> Vicar Collins. Of De Burgh Province.
> Conceited. Pompous. Narrow-minded.
> Silly. Still sucking up, I see,
> to the royal kings and ladies.
> How dreadful.

> LESLIE
> But where's your dignity, Darcy? Is he
> not found in your circles at times?
> Defend him.

> DARCY
> Leslie, I am in no humor ever, to give
> consequence to men who are slighted
> by female novelists.

> LESLIE
> That proud, is he?

> DARCY
> Tommy is at the plate now. This is a
> rare one, ladies and gentlemen.
> Rival siblings going at each other.
> One on the mound going for her
> second consecutive shutout. And one
> at the plate going for forty-three
> games with a hit in each.

> JANE AUSTEN
> Both sports royalty. Beloved by the fans.
> Dare I say, subjects.

> DARCY
> You surprise me, Jane. With my pride,
> I never imagined this: you, a fan,
> following ball.

> LESLIE
> Eyeing the plate; selecting her pitch;
> and now staring Tommy down. Eyes
> intense. Building. Focusing. Ready.
> Hiding her hand grip. Disguising
> her pitch. Bringing the ball and

LESLIE (CON'T)
skinny arms together. Winding up.
Rotating back.
Knee snapping up to the chin.

DARCY
And there's the throw.

LESLIE
Strike. Excellent form! Unbelievable
control, speed, power. That was a 105-
mile-an-hour fastball, and that's
just sailed inches from Master Tommy's
royal head.

JANE AUSTEN
I'm fond of saying, "It isn't what
we say or think that defines us
but what we do."
The peasant crowd is loving it.

LESLIE
Indeed, but Tommy is steaming.
Ooh—keep the discipline, boy.

DARCY
It looks like he is pointing.
Yes, he is pointing
in the direction of the
stained-glass front window
of the church directly over
the left-field battlements.

LESLIE
Oh, look in the royal box seats there.
Vicar has taken note.
Not pleased. Not pleased
at all. Take note, Jane Austen:
Vicar not pleased. Marauding crowd
loving it!

JANE AUSTEN
You gave me a character idea, Leslie.
Thank you.

DARCY
Back with the pitcher. Watch for
pretty Miss Polly's spitball.

LESLIE
Indeed. Good catch. It's illegal. Or
at least there's talk of that. But insiders
say they'll delay that decision perhaps
three hundred years.

JANE AUSTEN
But since she is the queen's daughter,
dare I offer some insight? No
umpire would dare call her out on that.

LESLIE
You're dead on.

DARCY
With the count now two balls and two
strikes, remember that there are no bats
used in this game. Only Tommy's
hand or arm is legal.

LESLIE
But look. She's winding up again—a little
hesitation there as she eyes the first pedestal
with those piercing blue eyes. Next, she's
going to home plate. And now, stockings,
ruffles all on display as she rotates her purple
and gold gown, twisting her petite body
around. Knee up, arms drawing back,
(VERY EXCITED)
sheer power on display and a little more
from pretty Miss Polly!

JANE AUSTEN
All of four feet tall.
I can see her left leg extending
a good three and a half feet in front
of her, stretching her petticoat to the
limit. It must be how
she's getting such power.

DARCY
And there it is: her sinker.
Curving up then straight down.

Suddenly we hear the -- SMACK – of Tommy hitting the ball using just his hand or arm.

> LESLIE
> But he clobbers it—Tommy does.
> Lovely ball. Lovely ball!

> DARCY
> Oh my. With that colossal hit,
> it looks like Tommy has snapped his
> own arm in two.

> LESLIE
> No big deal.
> It happens all the time.
> Turns boys into marauding men.
> Even knights of the realm,
> if you will.

> DARCY
> Tommy's rounding the bases now.

> JANE AUSTEN
> See. Not a bad name for a new sport.

> LESLIE
> But look there. Look at Polly run!

> JANE AUSTEN
> Dear diary. Note: Polly is waving off
> all the other adult players, for she
> is going for the ball herself.

> LESLIE
> Royal silk shoes, stockings not
> a problem. Not a problem at all.

> JANE AUSTEN
> My friend Elizabeth walks the fields
> while reading a good book. Finds it no
> trouble at all either. Why would Polly?

> DARCY
> It tells me she's not going to let
> Tommy damage her ERA or her
> win-and-loss legacy.

> DARCY (CON'T -- WITH EMPHASIS)
> Yes, for those new to the sport, you
> can put out the runner by striking
> that runner directly with the ball.
> I believe that that is what she
> is going to do.

> LESLIE
> She is closing in on the ball. It's in
> her petite fingers, and she
> fires it right at Tommy.

> JANE AUSTEN
> Smack into his face.

But Leslie is too excited to notice that there is an issue with Tommy, now face-down on the ground.

> LESLIE
> Another zinger!

> JANE AUSTEN
> A girl likes to cross and hammer
> it a little every now and again.

But Jane now sees that Tommy is down.

> LESLIE
> Legal play. By the book. He's out of there!

> DARCY
> Uh, Leslie?

> LESLIE
> That Polly—
> a regular Bo Jackson she is.

> DARCY
> Leslie!

> JANE AUSTEN
> Yes, Leslie.

> LESLIE
> That girl's got a cannon—
> all the way from the palace warning
> track she threw it.

> DARCY
> (SHOUTING IT)
> Leslie!!

> LESLIE
> (suddenly exasperated)
> What!!?

> DARCY
> Tommy is really out.
> I mean out cold.

> LESLIE
> Oh, dear. I see it now.
> Rather dormant, isn't he?

> DARCY
> While they're checking on him, Jane,
> besides your writing, what other
> things have you been up to?

> JANE AUSTEN
> Which of all my important nothings
> shall I tell you first?

> DARCY
> Tell us about that game you're forming.
> Rounders or something? Is that a game
> where you will use a stick or a cudgel
> to hit with instead of just your
> hand or arm?

But Leslie cuts in.

> LESLIE
> Why, I think Jane has an
> excellent idea. Excellent.
> Keep the purity of this ball
> game intact. While we let them
> set up that silly rounders thing. Then
> ship it off and send it to America or
> something like it to the towns over there.
> Maybe call it townball. Ha ha ha.
> But no offense intended to you, Jane.

> DARCY
> Careful, Leslie. We have a guest here
> with very strong opinions on the matter.

JANE AUSTEN
My good opinion, Leslie, once lost,
is lost forever.

DARCY
Yes. I hear that London publishers are
drooling to get into the US market.

LESLIE
For what do we live, but to make sport
of our neighbors and laugh at them
in our turn. Now that's a direct quote
from one of your novels, Miss Austen.

JANE AUSTEN
Heavens. Now I am vexed. Half agony.
Half hope. Apology. I have misjudged
you, Leslie.

LESLIE
Capital. Capital!

JANE AUSTEN
Still I must say, stupid men are
the only ones worth knowing, after all.

LESLIE
Ah, humor. I love you, Jane.

DARCY
Tommy is still down on the field. We are
sitting here most ardently impressed
with our guest commentator,
Miss Austen.

JANE AUSTEN
Where's the nearest hospital?

DARCY
Saint Giles.

LESLIE
Capital. Capital.

JANE AUSTEN
That is in Norwich, a hundred miles north.

LESLIE
Oh, heavens. Best be on their way.
A good three or four days' ride.

DARCY
Maybe so. I think this game is over.
Enjoyed color commentating,
did you, Jane?

JANE AUSTEN
I must learn to be content with
being happier than I deserve.
But must go. Bye.

Jane exits the booth while Darcy seems occupied with a producer stepping in with a book in hand.

LESLIE
Goodbye. Ha Ha Ha. She is a
tolerable one, that Jane is.

DARCY
And I'm just getting word. It is official. I
have just been handed the book. It reads
A Little Pretty Pocket Book, and now
they've added this: Intended for the
Instruction and Amusement of Little
Master Tommy and Pretty Miss Polly.
Oops. Where is she? I guess she is
coming back?

LESLIE
Is Jane the author?

DARCY
Austen? No. (PAUSE)
Well, that is it for us from
Hampton Court Palace Stadium
in London on this gentle
afternoon of July 4, 1744.

The booth and stadium torches go dark.

STADIUM WORKER (O.S.)
Lights out!

DARCY
(In the dark)
Miss Austen, in vain I have struggled.
It will not do. You must allow me
to tell you how ardently
I admire and love you.

LESLIE
Oh, Darcy. She's left the bloody booth
already. Stick to the ballgame.
Stick to baseball.

DARCY
Jane is too generous to trifle with me or
the notion of a new ballgame. My
affections for this game and her
are unchanged. But one word
from Jane will silence me on
this subject forever.

LESLIE
(losing it)
Give me a break, man! Get a manly
hold on yourself, Darcy. Try to
show a bit more selfish distain
for the feelings of others.
More arrogance. More conceit, man.
Women like her love that sort of thing!

END SCENE:

Thus ends our trip the stadium of your imagination.

Illustrations

Note: Technically, the Baseball Concept Model done in 2008 was also called America's Game Concept Model

Fig. 1: Baseball vs. bat illustration by Winston J Perez

Fig. 2: Boxing glove

Fig. 3: Baseball Concept Model, *Concerning the Nature and Structure of Concept*, by Winston J Perez, 2020, page 182

Fig. 4: Baseball Concept Model, Concerning the Nature and Structure of Concept, by Winston J Perez, 2020, page 187

Fig. 5: Taken from *Concerning the Nature and Structure of Concept*, by Winston J Perez, 2020 and the baseball concept model done in 2008

Fig. 6: Leather & attributes—Baseball Concept Model, by Winston J Perez, 2008

Fig. 7: Updated (2022) Baseball Concept Model by Winston J Perez

Fig. 8: Fin from 1963 Black Cadillac

Fig. 9: "The American Origin of Baseball" Illustration by Charles Reinhart, 1870

Fig. 10: A Little Pretty Pocket-book, John Newberry, 1744 Rare Book & Special Collections Division of the Library of Congress, Washington, DC

Fig. 11: Close up: A Little Pretty Pocket-book, by John Newberry, 1744 Rare Book & Special Collections Division of the Library of Congress, Washington, DC

Fig. 12: Base Ball Player's Pocket Companion, (Boston: Mayhew & Baker, 1859), page 31 Courtesy of Baseball Almanac, www.baseball-almanac.com

Fig. 13: The Rules for the Massachusetts Game (Town Ball), May 13,1858 Courtesy of Baseball Almanac, www.baseball-almanac.com

Fig. 14: Close up- The Rules for the Massachusetts Game (Town Ball), May 13,1858 Courtesy of Baseball Almanac, www.baseball-almanac.com

Fig. 15: Base Ball Player's Pocket Companion, (Boston: Mayhew & Baker, 1859) Courtesy of Baseball Almanac, www.baseball-almanac.com

Fig. 16: *The Boy's Own Book*, by William Clarke, Second Ed., 1828

Fig. 17: Rounder layouts is from The Boy's Own Book, by William Clarke, 1928; feeder layout from later editions. Dotted round circle added to feeder by Perez for emphasis

Fig. 18: "Exeter," (England) in Beauties of England and Wales, Artist Unknown

Fig. 19: Rounders shape taken from The Boy's Own Book, 1828; feeder shape to the right taken from later editions, with modifications (dotted line, and small c) made by author Perez

Fig. 20: Rounders layout taken from The Boy's Own Book, 1828; feeder layout taken from later editions

Fig. 21: The diamond shape above has been added for emphasis by author Perez. Also, Perez has removed the capital C and D found in the original feeder layout

Fig. 22: Baseball Glove Concept Model by Winston J Perez

Fig. 23: Baseball Base Concept Model, by Winston J Perez

Fig. 24: Baseball Concept Model, *Concerning the Nature and Structure of Concept*, 2020, page 188
Fig. 25: Baseball Bat Concept Model by Winston J Perez
Fig. 26: Baseball Stick-Bat Concept Model by Winston J Perez
Fig. 27: Baseball Strike Concept Model by Winston J Perez
Fig. 28: Conceptmodeling Baseball Card No. 3, by Winston Perez
Fig. 29: Baseball Pitching Concept Model by Winston J Perez
Fig. 30: Combined Baseball Concept Model by Winston J Perez

References & Books

Key Reference Book:
David Block, *Baseball before We Knew It: A Search for the Roots of the Game* (Bison Books, 2006).

Other Key References (Yes, the last one is mine, oh well):
John Newberry, *A Little Pretty Pocket-book, Intended for the Amusement of Little Master Tommy and Pretty Miss Polly with Two Letters from Jack The Giant Killer* (England: John Newberry, 1744).
William Clarke, *The Boy's Own Book*, (London: Vizetelly, Branston and Co.), 1828, Second Edition.
William Clarke, *The Boy's Own Book*, (London: D. Bogue, 1849).
The Base Ball Player's Pocket Companion, (Boston: Mathew & Baker, 1859).
The Rules for the Massachusetts Game (Town Ball), May 13, 1858.
"How Baseball Began—A Member of the Gotham Club of Fifty Years Ago Tells About It." San Francisco Examiner, Nov. 27, 1887.
Jane Austen, *Northanger Abbey*, (John Murray, Albemarie Street: 1817).
Winston J. Perez, *Concerning the Nature and Structure of Concept* (Los Angeles: Simmons Shutter House Publishing, 2020).

Other Reference Books & Articles:
John Thorn, *Baseball in the Garden of Eden: The Secret History of the Early Game* (New York: Simon & Schuster, 2012).

Referenced by Other Sources:
John Thorn, "1791 and All That: Baseball and the Berkshires," BaseBall: A Journal of the Early Game, Volume 1, Number 1, 119-126.

New York Times

Remarks on Children's Play, 1811 Illustration

Porter's Spirit of the Times, December 27, 1856, 276.

Robin Carver, *The Book of Sports,* (Boston: Lilly Wait, Colman and Holdman, 1934).

Geo P. Daniels, *The Boy's and Girls Book of Sports* (Providence: Geo P. Daniels, 1935)

S. Babcock, *The Boy's Book of Sports,* (New Haven: S. Babcock, 1935),

Online Sources:

Library of Congress

Encyclopedia Britannica,

New World Encyclopedia

Wikipedia

SABR.org

Baseball-reference.com

Reference.com

thefinancialexpress.com

Baseball-Almanac.com

stevetheump.com

Sportsnetla.com

thepostgame.com

Heritage Auctions, HA.com

Endnotes

1 David Block, *Baseball before We Knew It: A Search for the Roots of the Game* (Bison Books, 2006).
2 John Thorn, *Baseball in the Garden of Eden: The Secret History of the Early Game* (New York: Simon & Schuster, 2012).
3 Chris Silva, "The Fascinating History of a Baseball Glove," thepostgame.com, July 7, 2011
4 Cynthia Bir, The Science Behind Baseball, Sci Journer, March 2, 2012
5 Alan Schwarz, The Numbers Game,
6 Google search, "How was baseball invented?" which references Wikipedia https://en.wikipedia.org/wiki/History_of_baseball May 31, 22
7 Block's *Baseball Before We Knew It: A Search for the Roots of the Game*
8 "Rounders (English Game)," Encyclopedia Britannica, (Retrieved: August 8, 2021).
9 Jane Austin, *Northhanger Abbey,* 1818
10 "Baseball," New World Encyclopedia (Retrieved: February 16, 2022).
11 "Baseball," New World Encyclopedia (Retrieved: February 16, 2022).
12 "Cricket," Encyclopedia Britannica, (Retrieved: August 8, 2021).
13 "The Official History of Baseball," Major League Baseball Productions, Vol. 1, 1994.
14 "The Origins of Baseball," Baseball-reference.com, Cricket and Rounders Section, (Retrieved May 26, 2020).
15 "Rounders (English Game)," Wikipedia, (Retrieved: February 16, 2022).
16 "Rounders (English Game)," Wikipedia, (Retrieved: September 17, 2020).
17 "Baseball, A Film by Ken Burns" (National Endowments for the Arts, PBS, 1994).
18 "Baseball, A Film by Ken Burns" (National Endowments for the Arts, PBS, 1994).
19 "Baseball, A Film by Ken Burns" (National Endowments for the Arts, PBS, 1994).
20 The Miriam and Ira D. Wallach Division of Art, Prints and Photographs: Photography Collection, The New York Public Library. "The American origin of baseball" By Charles Stanley Reinhart, New York Public Library Digital Collections/ (Accessed June 19, 2022).
21 "Baseball, A Film by Ken Burns" (National Endowments for the Arts, PBS, 1994).
22 *The Base Ball Player's Pocket Companion,* (Boston: Mathew & Baker, 1859), 31.
23 *The Rules for the Massachusetts Game (Town Ball)* from 1858.

24 *The Rules for the Massachusetts Game (Town Ball)* from 1858.
25 *The Rules for the Massachusetts Game (Town Ball)* from 1858.
26 "Baseball, A Film by Ken Burns" (National Endowments for the Arts, PBS, 1994)
27 "Baseball, A Film by Ken Burns" (National Endowments for the Arts, PBS, 1994)
28 "How Baseball Began—A Member of the Gotham Club of Fifty Years Ago Tells About It." San Francisco Examiner, November 27, 1887.
29 "How Baseball Began—A Member of the Gotham Club of Fifty Years Ago Tells About It." San Francisco Examiner, November 27, 1887.
30 "Baseball," "History," Encyclopedia Britannica, (First retrieved: August 8, 2021, again April, 2022) https://www.britannica.com/sports/baseball/History.
31 William Clarke, *The Boy's Own Book*, (London: Vizetelly, Branston and Co.), 1828, Second Edition.
32 Andrew Schiff, "Henry Chadwick," SABR.org, Accessed February 26, 2022: https://sabr.org/bioproj/person/henry-chadwick/
33 Ward, John Montgomery, *Base-ball: How to Become a Player*, Philadelphia, The Athletic Publishing Company, 1888
34 Johann Christoph Friedrich Guthsmuth,
35 Bernie Mussill, The Evolution of the Baseball Bat, stevetheump.com, Accessed February 26, 2022: http://www.stevetheump.com/Bat_History.htm.
36 Jane Jacobs, *The Death and Life of Great American Cities*,
37 "How Baseball Began—A Member of the Gotham Club of Fifty Years Ago Tells About It." San Francisco Examiner, November 27, 1887.
38 "Ebbets Field Opening Victory for Superbas—30,000 Fans Jam Into New Home of Brooklyn Club—Yankees Lose, 3 to 2." New York Times, April 6, 1913, S1.
39 John Thorn, "1791 and All That: Baseball and the Berkshires," Base Ball: A journal of the Early Game, Volume 1, Number 1, 119-126
40 John Thorn, *Baseball in the Garden of Eden, The Secret History of the Early Game.* (New York: Simon and Schuster, 2012)
41 Winston J Perez, *Concerning the Nature and Structure of Concept*, 2020

Winston J. Perez

Baseball Concept Model Can Be Found In Winston's Concept Modeling Master Course

Winston Perez is the founder of the discipline of concept modeling. This book and his book *Concerning the Nature and Structure of Concept* are available online and through places such as Barnes and Noble, Amazon, or this website: www.conceptmodeling.com.

A walk through of the Baseball Concept Model can be found in Winston's concept modeling master course. For those interested in signing up for a course on concept modeling, it is called *Ideation and Concept Modeling Master Course*.

Winston guides subscribers through an explanation of concept modeling which includes parts of the Baseball Concept Model.
Email info@conceptmodeling.com for information.
Available online.

Copyright 2021-2023 Winston Perez
All rights reserved.

No portion of this book may be used in any manner without the express written permission of Winston Perez.

FADE TO BLACK: TUDOR DYNASTY MEMORIAL STADIUM
And we hear...

"Popcorn. Peanuts..... Disruptive Technology. Popcorn. Peanuts.....
  Disruptive Technology."

www.ingramcontent.com/pod-product-compliance
Lightning Source LLC
Chambersburg PA
CBHW070343010526
44119CB00029B/423/J